MACRAME
SOURCES OF FINE KNOT

edited by Jules & Kaethe Kliot

MW00679996

The knot as a decorative element permeates virtually every culture, taking different directions as manifested within these cultures. In the East, the knot became an entity in itself as a decorative element on every garment, sword and bag as well as any other object. The meticulously made kumihimo braided cords became the element for forming the knot, with the finished assembly as precious as any work of art.

In the West, the knot became the basic element for creating rhythms and patterns as it was joined by a myriad of other knots to form a directed pattern. While the continual knotting of a single cord could become the basis for terminating the free warp ends from a woven piece, it was the joining of adjacent warp ends in endless patterns that developed into one of the richest open-work lace techniques. Free from the woven pieces, threads could be added and deleted at will with this new technique now finding its parallels to the development of bobbin lace.

The name assigned to this multi-thread knotted lace technique was MACRAMÉ, a name with origins in early Near Eastern textiles where decorative knotted fringes terminated every tent, garment and towel— the Arabic word translated to mean a large fringed cloth.

Where Bobbin Lace, a related multi thread technique, relies solely on plaiting, Macramé relies solely on knotting. Both techniques rely on two basic motions—Bobbin Lace, the twist and cross; Macame, the hitch and half-hitch. Both techniques, while able to work with an unlimited number of threads, use only four threads, with exceptions, at any one time. Materials, however, are very different. Macramé requires a tightly twisted cord while bobbin lace requires a soft loosely twisted cord. The tightly twisted cords were referred to as "Macramé" cords and found use in other needle techniques such as crochet where the technique was referred to as Macramé Crochet. By the nature of the cord and the knot, Macramé would always have a relatively stiff texture lending itself more for decorative elements rather then costume. The knot was also more comfortable with geometric designs, rather than the free flowing designs which worked so well with the plaiting technique of bobbin lace. The knotted structure and the tightly twisted threads made this lace virtually indestructible, assuring it a continued presence for Church and household use where utility as well as beauty would remain a prime requirement.

Developing along with the other lace techniques in the 16th century, Macramé went in the same direction in terms of refinement and technique. In Italy, the lace was referred to as *punto a gruppo* where, working with finer and finer threads, pictorial as well as geometric patterns were executed. Fashion, however, dictated softness in lace, and Macramé soon succumbed to the more fashionable bobbin and needle lace techniques.

Along with the revival of so many other techniques in the latter part of the 19th century, Macramé, in its traditional forms, became one of the more popular textile techniques. Lending itself to the rich Victorian ornamentation of this period, Macramé would allow the worker, as related in *Sylvia's Book of Macramé Lace*,

> to "find herself able to work rich trimmings for black and coloured costumes both for home wear, garden parties, and seaside rambles—fairylike adornments for household and underlinen-fringes, edgings, and insertions for towels, pillows, antimacassars—covers for sofa-cushions, etc."

Many manuals were written in the 1880's all firmly asserting the newness of this art, some even claiming it as a "new invention." The enthusiasm lasted till the early 1900's with Macramé not gaining popularity again till the 1960's where it was again to be the first of an enthusiastic revival of forgotten textile techniques. Development was now more involved with crafts, with the practical hanging planter becoming synonymous with Macramé.

This volume reproduces some of the important and rare turn-of-the-century sources signaling the revival of Macramé as well as relevant works from the editor's collection.

CONTENTS

Note: Numbers in [ ] designate page numbers of this book. Other page references are from original publications and are retained for text continuity.

LACIS
PUBLICATIONS
3163 Adeline Street, Berkeley, CA 94703

© 1998, LACIS
This edition published 2005
ISBN 978-0-916896-97-3

MACRAMÉ — XVI CENTURY.

370

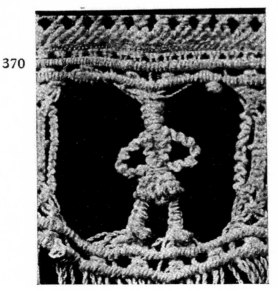

371

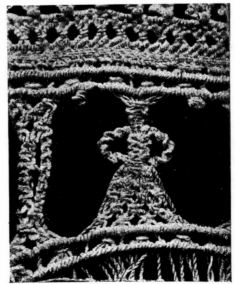

from OLD ITALIAN LACE, Elisa Ricci, 1913

SYLVIA'S

BOOK OF

MACRAMÉ LACE.

CONTAINING

ILLUSTRATIONS OF MANY NEW AND ORIGINAL DESIGNS,

WITH COMPLETE INSTRUCTIONS FOR WORKING, CHOICE OF MATERIALS, AND SUGGESTIONS FOR THEIR ADAPTATION.

WARD, LOCK, AND CO.

LONDON: WARWICK HOUSE, SALISBURY SQUARE, E.C.
NEW YORK : BOND STREET.

PREFACE.

———◇———

THIS kind of fancy work is not exactly a novelty, except in the sense that when anything becomes so old as to be forgotten, its revival has all the effect of a first appearance. It is a beautiful and effective lace, costing little difficulty to the worker, and useful in a variety of directions. It is an exceedingly fashionable occupation, and in addition to presenting our readers with the clearest instructions yet issued upon the subject, we have also the satisfaction of offering, in the present volume, the largest number and greatest variety of designs that have hitherto been collected together.

stitch; but when that is once done, she will find herself able to work rich trimmings for black and coloured costumes both for

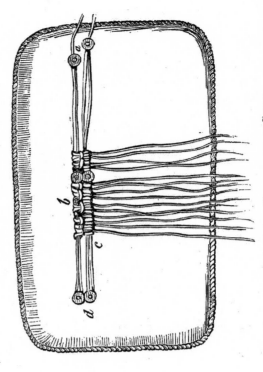

339.—MINIATURE CUSHION, WITH FOUNDATION THREAD, AND PUTTING ON OF THE STITCHES.

340.—FIRST ROW WITH A CORD.

home wear, garden parties, and seaside rambles—fairylike adornments for household and underlinen—fringes, edgings, and

290

MACRAMÉ LACE.

MODE OF WORKING.

Introduction—Materials—Cushions—Various Stitches—Knotted Bar—Star or Diamond—Genoese Knot—Solomon's Knot—Grounding.

THIS fascinating kind of fancy-work dates as far back as the fifteenth century. The materials are inexpensive, and the lace lasts almost for ever. The work progresses rapidly, and can be made in many materials; none, however, so good as the cord made and sold for the purpose. The manipulation consists in tying knots of various kinds. This lace can be unhesitatingly recommended as a pleasant occupation and pastime.

Goethe, somewhere or other, in exalting music above every other art, does so on the ground that it produces its marvellous effects with so little display of means and tools; and if this test be applied to our present work, it will rank very high amid the rival styles of lacemaking and embroidery. No dazzling range of colours, no blending of different materials, not even a thimble and needle, are wanted to produce the charming effects of our Macramé work.

And first of all, why "Macramé?" Macramé is nothing but the name given by the Italians round about Genoa (the home and birthplace of the work) to a coarse material used for towels, the fringed ends of which are knotted in several of the lace stitches which we shall afterwards explain. As to the materials required, they are of the simplest. We advise our fair reader to begin with the coarse Macramé thread until she has learnt how to wield her weapons, and thoroughly mastered every

289

U

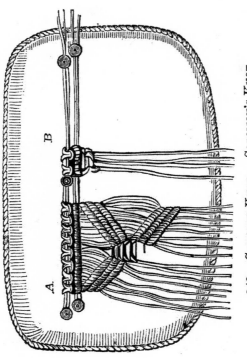

343.—GENOESE KNOT. SOLOMON'S KNOT.

Macramé Lace.

holland materials, filoselle for fancy trimmings, and so on in endless variety. But, being a beginner, she will at first try "her 'prentice hand" on the coarse Macramé thread generally preferred for trimming brackets, drawing-room tables, mantelpieces, etc.

The first thing wanted is a weighted cushion, measuring about ten inches long by seven or eight wide. The best way is to get a bag of coarse towelling of the dimensions above given, and stuff it carefully with sand and bran well mixed; the sand will give it the necessary weight, and the bran is easy to stick

pins in. As to the cover of the cushion, we strongly recommend a fine dark cloth; some people advise a striped material, such as ticking, saying that the lines are a help in stretching the horizontal threads, but in our opinion the lines are often rather confusing than helpful, and we believe our pupil will find them wholly unnecessary, while cloth is much pleasanter than ticking to work upon.

The cushion made, and slightly rounded at the top, the learner will provide herself with a box of steel toilet-pins with glass heads, sold for the purpose, and she will take care to have

292

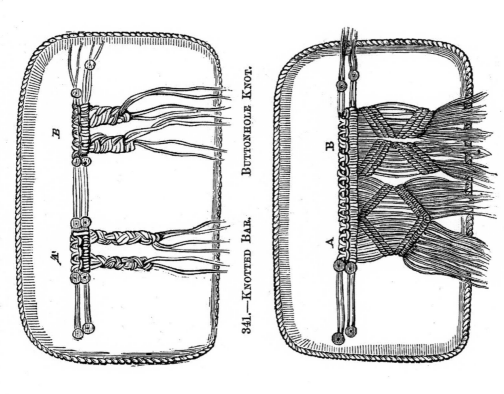

341.—KNOTTED BAR. BUTTONHOLE KNOT.

342.—DIAMOND AND STAR.

Uses of Macramé Lace.

insertions for towels, pillows, antimacassars—covers for soft cushions, etc., etc. For these latter purposes she will have t

her command black, white, and coloured silks made specially fo Macramé work, very fine flax thread for the white linen, brow grey, and all shades of écru for unbleached or coloured linen ar

291

First Stage.

them of bright colours, so as to make every process of her work gay and pretty. A piece of coarse thread, double the length of the lace required, is then folded in half, and pinned on the left side of the cushion as it faces the worker. This double thread is called the "foundation thread," and is pinned horizontally across the cushion. A number of doubled threads—say half a yard long when doubled—are cut ready and fastened on to the foundation thread, as shown in Illustration 339.

Look at the illustration, and having pinned the foundation

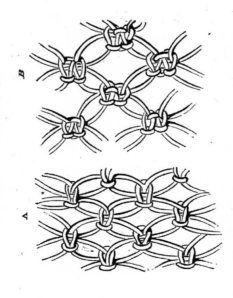

344.—DESIGNS FOR GROUNDING, OR OPEN KNOTTING.

thread as directed, take up one of the double lengths, and pass the doubled centre downwards under the foundation thread, so that the two ends are lying across the far side of the cushion; then bring these two ends through the loop you passed under the foundation thread, and draw up the stitch. The first row of every pattern is worked in this way by putting on as many threads as are wanted.

The next thing to be learnt is the Macramé knot, which enters into every pattern, and is used in marking what is called the cord—a pretty, close pattern, generally following close upon the first row of the work.

293

Macramé Lace.

The cord and Macramé knot illustrate each other, and are better learnt together. We suppose that the foundation thread is stretched upon the cushion, and the first row worked according to Illustration 339. Now consult Illustration 340.

You will notice that a second double foundation thread has been pinned on close to the stitches of the first row, and it is along this second thread that the cord is worked. The foun-

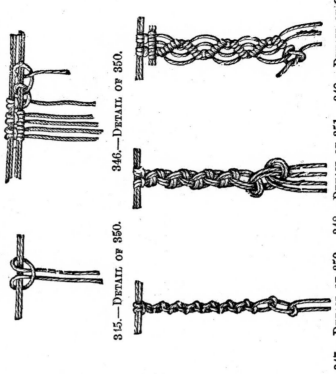

345.—DETAIL OF 350.   346.—DETAIL OF 350.

347.—DETAIL OF 350.   348.—DETAIL OF 351.   349.—DETAIL OF 352

dation thread is pinned at first only on the left side of the cushion, and must be held raised a little from the cushion in the right hand. Now take up in your left hand the first single vertical thread *, pass it over and then under the foundation thread and through the loop made by itself; draw up tight, and repeat from *. Proceed in the same manner with every thread in succession. Our illustration gives a useful hint to the learner by

294

Knotted Bar.

showing the use of pins to hold the stitches well in place and close together; and we may add that care should be taken not to split the thread, but to stick the pins between two threads; also to be careful to take the threads in their proper order. Having worked the cord, there only needs a word as to the Macramé knot. It is worked exactly as above described, the

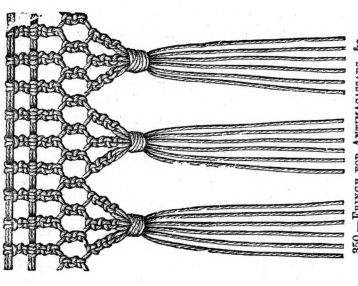

350.—FRINGE FOR ANTIMACASSARS, &c.

stitch being formed twice with the same vertical thread, as it is the second half of the stitch which holds the first in place.

We come now to the Knotted Bar. This is a useful stitch, and enters largely into all patterns. We again suppose the cushion before you, with its cord neatly worked along the second foundation row. Now consult Illustration 341.

You see that in the examples given four threads are used in

295

Macramé Lace.

each bar. Beginning, then, with Fig. A, work with the two left-hand threads a single or half Macramé knot over the next two threads, and then work the same knot with those threads over the first two. Repeat this alternately, and you will have accomplished the double Macramé knot shown in Fig. A. It is called double because it is worked with two threads, not bu-

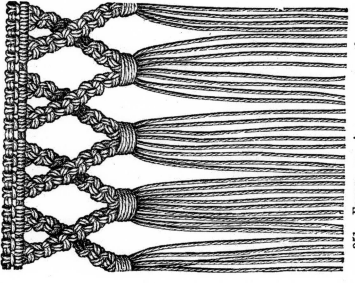

351.—FRINGE FOR ANTIMACASSARS, &c.

cause it is worked twice with the same threads. We give no further illustrations of this bar. Our fair pupil has already divined how it may be worked with single instead of double thread, with three over three, with half or complete Macramé knots, and so on. When she has exercised her skill in all these varieties she should turn to Fig. B, and work the buttonhole

296

Diamond or Star Pattern.

knot. Again four threads are required; take three threads in the left hand, in the right hand take up the fourth thread, pass it over and then under the three threads, and draw it up, this time not too tightly. The same remarks apply to this useful knot as to the one represented in the preceding figure; varia-

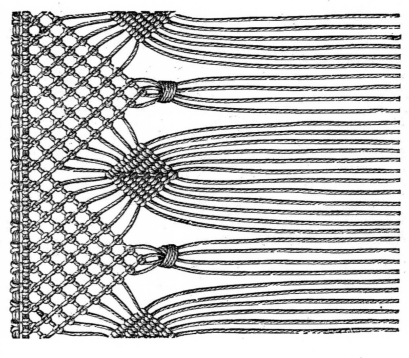

352.—FRINGE FOR ANTIMACASSARS, &c.

297

tions of it will be easily recognised in patterns of Macramé work, and will be copied without difficulty.

The next thing to be mastered is the Diamond or Star Pattern. We say "or," advisedly, for the one is but a variation of the other. On looking at the best styles of Macramé lace, it

Macramé Lace.

will be almost always found that this figure is worked immediately beneath the cord described in Illustration 340. We give, therefore, in the following diagram the usual heading of the preceding illustrations. Now consult Illustration 342.

Sixteen single vertical threads must be set aside for this

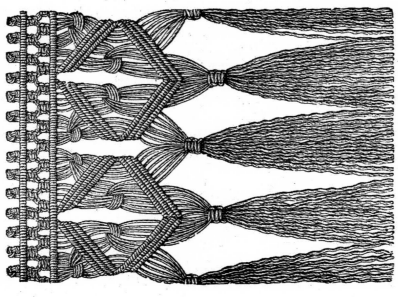

353.—FRINGE.

298

pattern; and for the present the eight right-hand threads had better be twisted round a pin, and fastened on to the cushion, out of the way. The pattern is now begun with the eight left-hand threads, as follows:—Take the eighth, or right hand, thread in your left hand, and hold it diagonally over the other seven close to the first, and work over it with every thread in succession a Macramé knot, as before, of course, taking in the thread which formed the leader in the last row. Now unpin your

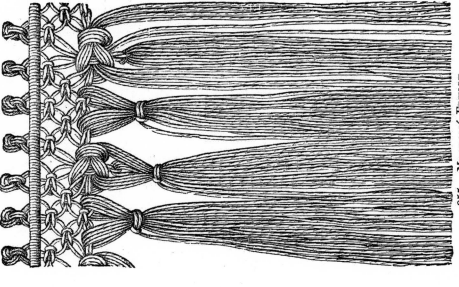

355.—MACRAMÉ FRINGE.

300

second group of eight threads. Take the first for the leader, and hold it diagonally across the other seven; take the second thread, and work a Macramé knot over the leader, do the same with every thread in succession, and pin down the leader as be-

Pattern of Fringe.

threads, letting it slope downwards at the angle shown in the diagram. This thread is technically known as the "leader:" it is better to keep the term "foundation" threads for the horizontal ones. Now take the seventh thread in your right hand, and work over the leader a complete Macramé knot, keeping the

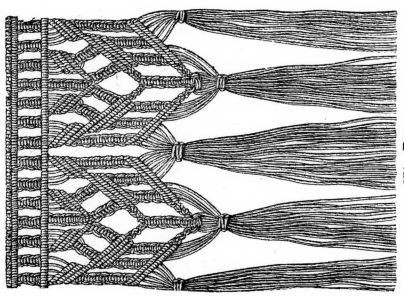

354.—FRINGE.

299

leader carefully in position. Repeat the Macramé knot with every thread in succession down to the first, and pin the leader to the cushion. In some patterns only one leader is used, but, as our diagram represents a double diamond, you will now take the seventh or right-hand thread as a second leader; place it

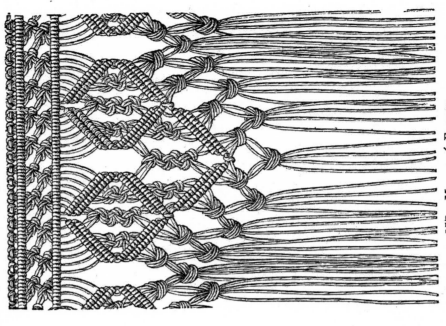

357.—MACRAMÉ FRINGE.

302

Macramé Lace.

the second thread as leader, working over it the second row. To finish the diamond, take the outer right-hand thread of the second group, and slant it down to the centre, work over it the row of Macramé knots; then take what is now the outer right-hand thread as leader, and work the second row. Lastly, tie the two centre threads together in a Macramé knot. By this time, we hope, the diamond is a complete success, and that our fair reader is already devising many an original combination to

356.—MACRAMÉ FRINGE.

301

Macramé Fringe.

fore. Then take the second thread for your leader, and work over it the second row of Macramé knots. By this time you will see that the upper half of your diamond is achieved. Use pins freely in this part of the work, that your diamond may be true and firm. Now take the first left-hand thread as leader, slant it downward to the centre of the diamond over the other seven threads, and work your row of Macramé knots; then use

Macramé Lace.

nation they occur they may present no difficulty. Very pretty
ntres are often worked in these diamonds with several of the
dinary lace stitches, and in our next diagram we give one of

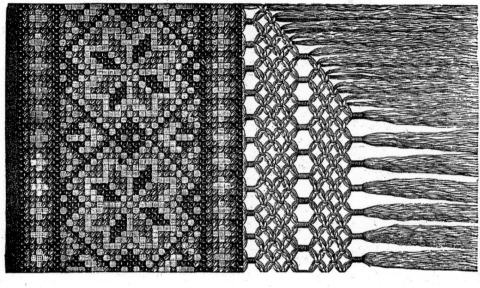

359.—Fringe. (Cross-stitch and Macramé.)

e prettiest and most useful. It is generally known as the
alian or Genoese knot.

304

[pages 305-336 of original manuscript omitted from this book.]

Fringe.

vary the one just worked out as an example. As to the star, it
is nothing but a diamond reversed—that is, it is begun with the
first, or left hand, thread as a leader, and when half completed
it is joined in the centre by tying two threads in a Macramé

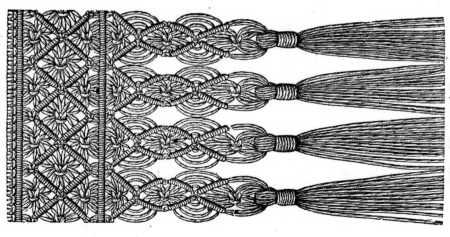

358.—Macramé Fringe.

knot, as we directed in describing the diamond pattern. The
three diagonal lines in Fig. B will often be claimed as old
acquaintances in Macramé lace, although they may form no part
of either star or diamond, and we hope that in whatever com-

303

[11]

INSERTIONS.

For Underlinen—Trimmings—Furniture.

Nos. 371 and 372. Insertions. (Macramé Work.) These two patterns look best when knotted with very fine thread. No. 371 is worked the long way, and is begun by tying double threads, of a yard long, to a double foundation thread. 1st row: Over a doubled horizontal thread, laid across the knotted strands, work 2 buttonhole-knots with every strand. 2nd row: 1 double knot with every 4 strands. 3rd row: Like the 1st row. 4th row: Measure the distances from the illustration, and remember that the strands are numbered according to their *apparent* order in the course of the work. For one diagonal pattern take 6 strands, 3 times alternately place the 6th strand aslant over the 5th, 4th, 3rd, 2nd, and 1st, and work over it 2 buttonhole loops with each of the latter in succession. 5th row: Like the 1st. 6th row: Like the 4th, but in reversed position. 7th to 9th rows: Like the 1st to the 3rd. 10th row: With 16 strands. To form the diamond, place twice alternately the 8th strand diagonally across the other 7, and with the latter work 2 buttonhole loops over the diagonal line; then work the same pattern in reversed position with the 9th to the 16th strands; then with the centre 12 strands, taking the first 3 and the last 3 together, and working with them 1 double knot over the other 6; then 2 patterns in reversed position, according to the illustration. The 4 knotted bars also take 16 strands, 4 to each bar; 6 times alternately 1 buttonhole knot with the 1st and 2nd end together over the 3rd and 4th together, and one buttonhole knot with the latter over the 1st and 2nd. When this row is finished, repeat 9 rows like the first 9, in reversed position. The projecting threads are then

337

fastened on the wrong side and cut off. For No. 372, tie a number of strands to a doubled foundation thread; miss 2 strands, take the 3rd strand and tie it to the foundation thread *before*

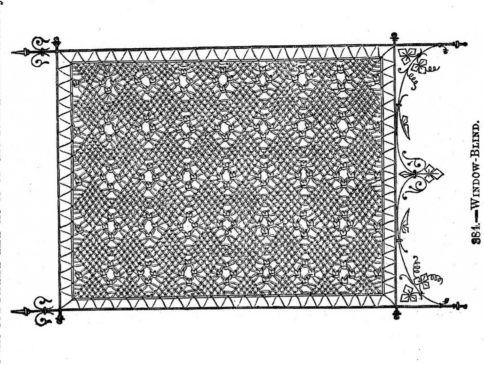

364.—WINDOW-BLIND.

the preceding 2 strands, so as to form a loop (working from right to left), and work 14 buttonhole loops over it with the other end of the same thread; then **work** over the foundation thread 2 buttonhole loops with the 2 threads; repeat so as to form the

838

[12]

Macramé Lace.

reversed position. 8th row: With 28 strands place the 14th strand diagonally across the 13th to the 1st, and work in succession.

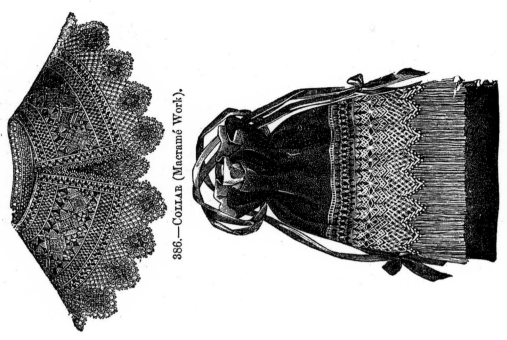

336.—Collar (Macramé Work).

Detail of Window-Blind.

row of loops shown in the illustration. 1st row: Over a double foundation thread, 2 buttonhole loops, with each strand in succession. 2nd row: 1 double knot with every 4 threads. 3rd

385.—Detail of 334.

row: 4 buttonhole loops, with the 1st over the 2nd, and the 4th over the 3rd of every 4 strands. 4th row: 1 double knot, with the 3rd and 4th end of 1 pattern and the 1st and 2nd of the next. 5th to 7th row: Like the 3rd to the 1st, but in

339

387.—Work-Bag.

sion 2 buttonhole knots over it with each thread; then proceed in the same way, but in reversed position, with the 15th strand placed across the 16th to the 28th; then 12 double

340

Macramé Lace.

knots each with the 3rd to the 6th, the 7th to the 10th, the 11th to the 14th, the 15th to the 18th, the 19th to the 22nd, and the 23rd to the 26th. These knots are crossed, as shown in the illustration, and 1 double knot is worked with the 2 last strands of one and the two first of the following knot. Then work 2 diagonal lines as before, and the square is completed. The 8 rows which follow are like those at the beginning of the pattern; the projecting threads are then fastened down on the wrong side, and cut off.

No. 373. Various Purposes. (Macramé Work.) According to the use for which this is assigned, the insertion may be worked either in strong silk, thread, or tapestry wool. A number of strands, about 20 inches long, are folded in half, and knotted together once. Each of these knots is fastened with a pin to the weighted cushion, at the distance shown in No. 373. 1st row: Place a double foundation thread horizontally across the strands, and work over it 2 buttonhole knots with each strand in succession. 2nd row: (each pattern requires 4 threads) *, 2 buttonhole knots with the 4th of the first 4 strands over the centre 2, 2 buttonhole knots with the first strand over the centre 2, repeat from *. 3rd row: Like the first row. 4th row (each pattern requires 24 strands): Twice alternately place the first of the 24 strands aslant over the 2nd to the 12th, and work over it 2 buttonhole knots with each strand in succession, then with the remaining 12 strands work a similar pattern, but in reverse position, using the 24th strand as a foundation thread. 5th row: * 1 raised spot as follows: 4½ double knots, with the 23rd and 24th strands of 1 pattern, and the 1st and 2nd of the next, then thread the first of these 4 strands between the 23rd and 24th of the 4th strand, between the 1st and 2nd strands, from which the 4½ double knots started, draw the strands tight, and work half a double knot, then, consulting the illustration, place the 9th, 10th, 11th, and 12th of the 24 strands over the 13th, 14th, 15th, and 16th, and under the 17th, 18th, 19th, and

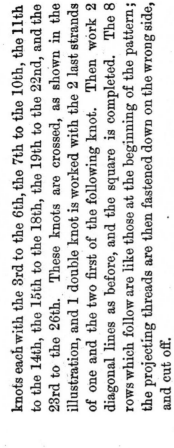

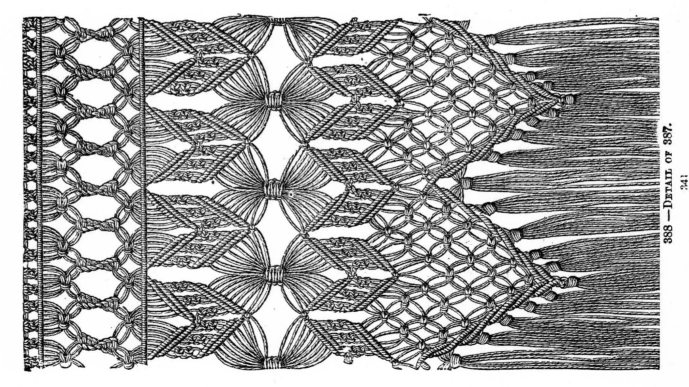

388.—Detail of 387.

341

342

Macrame Lace.

Pattern for Collars.

cushion, and a double foundation thread is laid across the strands. Then work from left to right as follows ;—1st row:

382.—DETAIL OF 386.

1.5

Woollen Fringe.

20th, and place the 5th, 6th, 7th, and 8th strands under the 13th, 14th, 15th, and 16th, and over the 17th, 18th, 19th, and 20th strands, repeat from *. 6th row: Like the 4th, but the pattern must occur in reversed position. 7th to 9th rows: Like the 1st to the 3rd and 10th row, 1 buttonhole knot with the 3rd and 4th strands over the 1st and 2nd, repeat. Then turn back the ends, fasten carefully, and cut them close to the work.

No. 374. Insertion. (Macramé Work.) Our model is knotted with tapestry wool as follows: Fold in half a number of strands 16 inches long, and tie each in a double buttonhole knot, taking of course two doubled strands and making with the first two a buttonhole knot over the last two, and then vice versâ. These knots are then pinned on to a weighted cushion at the distances shown in No. 374, and a double foundation thread is laid across them. 1st row: 2 buttonhole knots with each strand in succession over the foundation. 2nd row: 2 double knots with every 4 strands. 3rd row: Like the 1st. 4th row: * Every 4 of the next 16 strands are put together to form one strand, pass the 3rd of these strands under the 2nd and over the 1st, the 4th over the 2nd and under the 1st, † twice alternately place the 8th end slantwise across the 7th to the 1st and work 2 buttonhole loops with each in succession over the first, then repeat once from †, and then from *. 5th to 8th rows: Like the 3rd and 4th alternately, but the pattern of the even numbered row must occur in reversed position. 9th and 10th rows: Like the 2nd and 1st. 11th row: 1 double buttonhole knot with every 4 strands. The ends are then turned back, and fastened down on the wrong side and cut off close.

No. 375. Insertion. (Macramé Work.) Fold in half a sufficient number of strands of unbleached thread about 16 inches long, taking care that the number is divisible by eight. Then tie together every 4 strands, making a loop with the 3rd and 4th over the 1st and 2nd, and with the 1st and 2nd over the 3rd and 4th. Each loop is then pinned on to a weighted

Macramé Lace.

2 buttonhole loops over the foundation thread with every strand in succession. 2nd row: 1 buttonhole loop with the 3rd and 4th of every 4 strands over the 1st and 2nd, and 1 buttonhole loop with the 1st and 2nd over the 3rd and 4th. 3rd row: Like the 1st row. 4th row: * 4 double knots with the 1st to the 4th of the first 16 strands, 3 double knots with the 5th to the 8th, 2 double knots with the 9th to the 12th, and 3 double knots with the 13th to the 16th, repeat from *. 5th row: Leave the first two strands unnoticed, * twice alternately place the 8th of the next 16 strands in a slanting direction across the 7th to the 1st strand, and make 2 buttonhole loops with each of the latter in succession over the 8th strand, twice alternately place the 9th strand in a slanting direction over the 10th to the 16th, and work 2 similar loops with each over the 9th strand, repeat from *. 6th row: Like the 5th, but in reversed position (see illustration as to crossing the strands of each pattern). 7th to 10th rows: Like the 4th to the 1st; but in reversed order of rows. 11th row: Like the 2nd row. Then turn back the 4 strands of every knot, and sew them firmly on the wrong side. The projecting strands are cut away.

No. 376. Insertion for Underlinen. (Knotted Work.) Take 12 strands of thread two yards long and fold them in halves. 1st row: 4 tatted knots with the 1st over the 2nd, the 4th over the 3rd, the 21st over the 22nd, and the 24th over the 23rd; then 1 double knot with the first 4, the centre 4, and the last 4; 4 tatted knots with the 5th over the 6th, and the 20th over the 19th; 3 tatted knots with the 7th over the 8th, and the 18th over the 17th; 1 tatted knot with the 9th over the 10th, and the 16th over the 15th. 2nd row: 2 buttonhole knots with the 11th, 10th, 9th, 8th, 7th, 6th, and 5th strand in succession over the 12th strand, and 2 buttonhole knots with the 14th to the 20th over the 13th. Leave the first and last 4 unnoticed. 3rd to 8th row: Like the preceding, using as foundation thread the strand nearest to the beginning, and the strand used in one row is left

VARIOUS HOUSEHOLD ARTICLES.

Window-Drapery—Towels—Window-Blind—Work-Bag—Basket for Layette—Watch-Pocket.

Nos. 377 to 379. Window-Drapery. Long muslin curtains under curtains of brown rep, which have a border embroidered

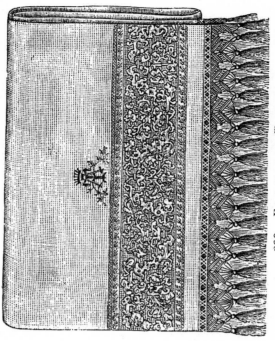

380.—Embroidered Towel.

348

on canvas in cross stitch. The design is worked with the following colours:—Etruscan red, yellow, pale blue, light red in wool and filoselle. The rep curtains have also a fringe and tassels of brown wool. White blind of fine holland slightly reeved, and alternating with strips of open knotted work. The lower edg of the blind has a border of the same work above a white fringe. For the knotted work see Illustration 377. Along a double foundation thread tie 34 strands of white cord about two yards

847

unnoticed in the following one, so that in the 8th row only 2 buttonhole loops are knotted. 9th row: 1 tatted knot with the 1st over the 2nd, and the 24th over the 23rd, 14 tatted knots with the 4th over the 3rd, and the 21st over the 22nd, 1 purl between the centre 2 of the 14; then 1 double knot with the first and last 4 close to the separate tatted knots, so as to form a loop with each, 2 buttonhole knots with the 6th to the 12th strand in succession over the 5th, and with the 19th to the 13th over the 20th, but before knotting this row draw the 5th and 20th strand through the purl of the loop. 10th row: 1 double knot with the 11th to the 14th strand, 7 times alternately 1 buttonhole knot with the 12th over the 11th, 1 with the 11th over the 12th, and 1 with the 13th over the 14th strand, then 1 double knot with the 4 centre strands, 15 tatted knots with the 9th over the 10th, and the 16th over the 15th strands, 1 purl between the 3rd and 4th, 6th and 7th, 9th and 10th, and 12th and 13th, 20 tatted knots with the 7th over the 8th, and the 18th over the 17th, joining the foundation thread to the nearest purl after the 4th knot (see illustration), and working 1 purl between the 6th and 7th, 10th and 11th, 14th and 15th knots, 25 tatted knots with the 5th over the 6th, and with the 20th over the 19th strand, joining to the purl after the 7th, 13th, and 19th tatted knots, and working 1 purl between the 9th and 10th, and 15th and 16th, * 7 tatted knots with the 1st over the 2nd, and with the 24th over the 23rd, 7 tatted knots with the 4th over the 3rd, and the 21st over the 22nd, joining to the purl after the 4th knot, 5 double knots with the first and last 4 strands. Repeat once more from *, pass the 4th and 21st strand through the nearest purls, and work 1 instead of 5 double knots with the first and last 4 strands. Repeat the 2nd to the 10th row as often as necessary.

Macramé Lace.

from †, then 2 buttonhole knots over the 30th strand with the 31st, 32nd, 33rd, and 34th strands successively; repeat the 2nd and 3rd rows as often as necessary, and finish off with a row like

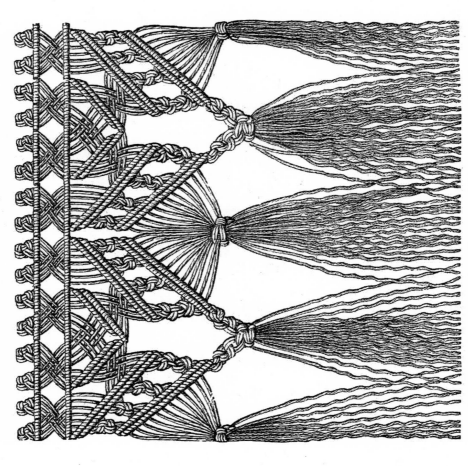

392.—DETAIL OF 390.

350

the 1st. For the border and fringe see Illustration 379. Knot 8 strands about 2 yards in length to a cord which is passed in the course of the work through the border, the latter being worked the narrow way. The beginning of this cord must be on

Towel with Fringe.

and a quarter in length. 1st row (from left to right): Along a horizontal cord, 2 buttonhole loops with each strand. 2nd row: Regulate the interval according to the illustration: 2 buttonhole loops with the 2nd, 3rd, 4th, and 5th strand successively over the 1st strand, † 5 tatted knots with the next strand over the 2 following, 5 tatted knots with the next strand but 3 over the 2nd strand *before* it, joining as shown in the illustration; repeat 3 times from †, then 2 buttonhole loops over the last

391.—EMBROIDERED TOWEL.

strand with the 33rd, 32nd, 31st, and 30th strands successively 3rd row: 2 buttonhole loops over the 5th strand with the 4th 3rd, 2nd, and 1st strands successively, † the next and the next strand but 4 are left unnoticed, with the 4 strands between proceed as follows:—Leave the 2 centre for the foundation and knot 2 double knots over them with the 1st and 4th; to form the raised spot join the outside strand of the 4 to the beginning of the knotted row, pulling through the ends with a crochet needle, and knotting 1 double knot close to it; repeat 3 time

349

Macramé Lace.

row (right to left): Like the 1st row. 3rd row (left to right):
† 5 tatted knots with the 1st strand over the 2nd and 3rd, then

394.—DETAIL OF 391.

352

with the next strand but 2, 3 tatted knots over the 2 preceding
strands; repeat once more from † 7 double knots with the last 4
strands with 1 double purl between the 1st and 2nd, 3rd and

Pattern for Towel.

the right side of the border. 1st row (from left to right): 2

393.—DETAIL OF 391.

351

buttonhole loops over the cord with each of the 16 strands. 2nd.

preceding. The interval of the foundation cord which forms the scallop must be measured from the illustration; repeat from †. 6th row: Like the 1st row; repeat the 2nd to the 6th row as often as necessary, then join to every scallop of the border 6 strands of 16 inches in length. 1st row: 3 tatted knots with the 1st over the 2nd and 3 with the 4th over the 3rd; repeat. 2nd row: 1 double knot with every 4 strands. 3rd row: Leave the 2 first strands unnoticed,* twice alternately 3 tatted knots with the 1st over the 2nd and the 4th over the 3rd, then with the last 2 of one pattern and the first 2 of the next 1 raised spot; repeat from *. 4th row: 1 double knot with the first 4 of the centre 8 strands, the others left unnoticed. 5th row: 1 raised spot with the centre 4 strands of every pattern, then knot together every 2 strands; see illustration, and cut the fringe even.

Nos. 380 to 383. Towel-Horse and Towel. (Macramé Work). Stand of black polished wood. Towel of coarse cloth worked with red thread according to Illustration 383. Four threads of the ground are required for one stitch. The pattern must be carefully worked, and then the right and wrong sides will be exactly alike. The centre of the border has also a monogram in the same stitch. The pattern given in Illustration 382 may be used instead. The edges of the towel are fringed and knotted in the pattern shown in Illustration 380. Tie every 12 strands in a knot, and before tying the 1st, 7th, and 12th of every division, pass a double strand of blue thread through the work, then divide the 12 strands in half, 4 double knots with every 4 of the 12 white strands, forming purls as shown in the illustration. 4 double knots with each 4 of the centre 8 strands, 4 double knots with the centre 4, then on each side of the pattern, using the white threads for the foundation, and taking in as required, the strands left unnoticed, 24 double knots with the blue threads on each side, consulting the illustration as to forming the purls and measuring the distances.

354

Pattern for Towel.

4th, and 5th and 6th. 4th row: † Leave the 1st and 6th strands untouched, 1 raised spot as before with the 4 centre strands;

895.—DETAIL OF 391.

353

repeat once more from †. The last 4 strands are left unnoticed. 5th row: † 3 tatted knots with the next strand over the 2nd next ones, 3 tatted knots with the next strand but 3, over the 2

2 A

Window-Blind.

Nos. 384 and 385. Window-Blind. (Macramé.) This pattern, of which No. 385 gives a section in the original size, is begun as follows:—Cut a double foundation thread equal in length to the circumference of the frame and begin at the upper edge, which must measure one-fourth of the whole. Fold a number of strands, 2 yards long, in half, and tie them in the ordinary way to the foundation thread, taking care that the number is divisible by 12. Every pattern takes 24 strands, but the reverse rows begin and end with half a pattern worked with 12 strands. 1st row: Leave the 1st and last 12 strands unnoticed; then 1 double knot with the centre 4 of the next 24 strands; repeat all along the row, and then 1 buttonhole loop with the 1st of the first 12 and 12th of the last 12 over the foundation thread as follows:— Work 1 buttonhole loop from above downward, and then the 2nd from above upward over the foundation thread at the sides of the work. (See No. 385.) These buttonhole stitches are worked in every row. In the 2nd, 3rd, and 4th rows work 2, 3, and 4 double knots with the centre 8, 12, and 16 strands respectively; but in the 2nd row, 1 double knot with the first 4 of the 1st 12 and the last 4 of the last 12. In the 3rd row work the double knot with the 3rd to the 6th of the first 12, and the 7th to the 10th of the last 12. In the 4th row the double knots are worked with the 1st to the 4th and 5th to the 8th of the first 12, and with the 5th to the 8th and the 9th to the 12th of the last 12. 5th row: For one knotted pattern proceed as follows: 1 buttonhole loop with the last 4 strands of one pattern together over the first 4 of the next pattern; then with the latter over the former, 5 double knots with the centre 20 strands; repeat from *. Then 1 double knot with the 3rd to the 6th and the 7th to the 10th of the first and last 12 strands. 6th to the 8th rows: 1 double knot with every 4 strands; but the pattern must occur in reversed position. 9th row: Like the 5th, only that the knotted pattern is worked *after* the double knots. 10th and 11th rows: Like the 4th and 3rd. 12th row: 1 knotted pattern

355

Macramé Lace.

like that of the 5th row with the last 8 strands of one pattern and the first of the next; then a similar knotted pattern with the last 4 of one pattern and the first 4 of the next: continue like the 2nd row. Now repeat as often as necessary the 1st to the 12th row. Then work another row like the first, and one in

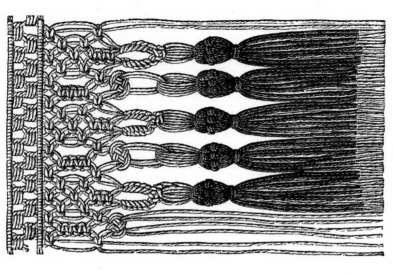

396.—Fringe for Towel.

which 2 buttonhole stitches are worked in succession over the foundation thread.

Nos. 386 and 389. Collar. (Macramé Work.) Worked with cream-coloured silk. Tie 159 strands, folded in half, and measuring 2 yards in length, to a double foundation thread about 10 inches long. After tying the strand to the foundation,

356

[21]

Macramé Lace.

like that of the 5th row with the last 8 strands of one pattern and the first 4 of the next; then a similar knotted pattern with the last 4 of one pattern and the first 4 of the next: continue like the 2nd row. Now repeat as often as necessary the 1st to in succession over a double foundation thread placed close under the first. Then work another row like the first, and one in the 12th row.

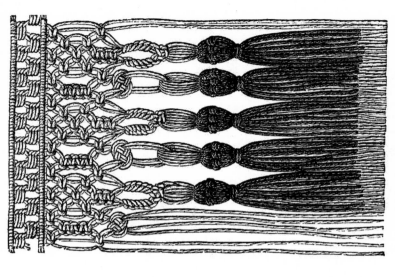

396.—Fringe for Towel.

355

Nos. 386 and 389. Collar. (Macramé Work.) Worked with cream-coloured silk. Tie 159 strands, folded in half, and measuring 2 yards in length, to a double foundation thread about 10 inches long. After tying the strand to the foundation,

356

which 2 buttonhole stitches are worked in succession over the foundation thread.

Collar.

work close to the knot with 1 strand over the foundation thread a buttonhole knot as follows:—1 buttonhole loop from above downwards and from below upwards, working from right to left. 1st row: 2 buttonhole knots with each strand in succession over a double foundation thread placed close under the first. 2nd row: The intervals must be measured according to the illustration, and the strands numbered in the order in which they occur. With 6 strands, 3 times alternately place the 1st strand aslant over the 2nd to the 6th and work over it 2 buttonhole knots with each strand. In the 3rd repetition of this row work 4 buttonhole knots with the last thread over the strand used as a foundation. 3rd row: Like the preceding, but work the pattern in reversed position with the last 3 strands of one figure and the first 3 of the next, copying the beginning and ends of the rows as shown in No. 389, which gives a section of the collar in the original size, adding new strands as they are required to make the slanting line of the front of the collar. 4th row: Like the 1st row. 5th row: * 4 button-hole loops from below upward with the 1st of the 4 strands over the 2nd, 4 buttonhole loops with the 4th over the 3rd, then 2 buttonhole loops with the 3rd over the 2nd, then 4 buttonhole loops with the 4th over the 2nd, then 4 buttonhole loops with the 2nd corresponding strands, 2 buttonhole loops with the 2nd over the 3rd strand; repeat from *. 6th to 8th rows: Like the preceding, but in reversed position, and at the end of the 8th row 2 knotted rows like the first 2 in the 5th row. 9th row: Like the 1st row. 10th row: * 7 chain knots as follows (1 buttonhole loop with the 1st over the 2nd strand, and then with the 2nd over the 1st):—8 chain knots with the 3rd and 4th strands, 9 chain knots with the 5th and 6th strands, 4 times alternately place the 7th strand aslant over the 8th to the 12th and work in succession 2 buttonhole loops over it with each strand, then work a similar pattern in reverse position with the 13th to the 18th strands, then 9 chain knots with the 19th and

357

Macramé Lace.

reversed position; repeat from *. 14th row: * Twice alternately place the 6th strand over the 5th to the 1st and work over it 2 buttonhole knots with each in succession, then 1 raised spot as before with the 1st and 2nd strand over 2 new short strands tied on as a foundation, then twice alternately place the 1st strand over the 2nd to the 6th and work over it 2 buttonhole loops with each strand, then knot a similar pattern in reversed position with the 31st to the 36th, and work the raised spot with the last 2 strands of one pattern and the first 2 of the next, but not until the first knotted row of the 2nd pattern has been worked; then consult the illustration, and by its help and that of the description already given work the centre pattern of the principal figure. The next 13 rows are like the first 13 but in reverse order; the rows of chain knots in the 16th to the 18th rows must be worked according to the illustration, and the last 4 rows must be continued to form the front of the collar, adding new strands as required by the shape. The 2 strands added to the lower edge of the border in the last row must be knotted just after the 6th strand has been tied, and are tied with 2 buttonhole loops over the foundation threads. 28th row: * 1 double knot with every 8 strands, using the centre 4 as a foundation, then 2 chain knots with the first 4, taking in 2 at a time, 2 chain knots with the last 4, taking in 2 at a time; repeat from *. 29th and 30th rows: Like the preceding, but the pattern must occur in reversed position, and at the beginning of the 30th row, after having worked the double knot of the 3rd and 4th patterns, and then always after the double knot of the 5th and 6th patterns, 2 rows of chain knots 4 in each row, and 2 knots with every 2 strands. 31st row: * For a medallion pattern. With the centre 12 of 48 strands. Place the 24th strand over the 25th to the 30th and work over it 2 buttonhole loops with each strand, place the 25th over the 23rd to the 19th and work over it 2 buttonhole loops with each strand, the 24th over the 26th

360

398.—Detail of 397.

Pattern for Bag.

over the new ones. 12th row: * 6 rows of chain knots with the first 12 of the 36 strands as follows:—9, 8, 7, and then 3 times 6 chain knots, then 4 times alternately place the 18th strand aslant over the 17th to the 13th, and work over it 2 buttonhole loops in succession with each strand, then work the same pattern in reversed position with the 19th to the 24th, then 6 rows of chain knots like the former but in reverse order with the 25th

to the 36th strand; repeat from *. 13th row: Place the 13th strand aslant across the 12th to the 1st and work over it 2 buttonhole loops with each strand, then 12 times place the next of the first 12 (the 12th first) aslant over the 14th to the 17th and work over it 2 buttonhole knots in succession with each strand, then place the 18th strand over the 12 which were used before as the foundation thread, and work over it 2 buttonhole knots with each in succession, then work a similar pattern in

359

Work-Bag.

to the 30th and work over it 2 buttonhole loops with each strand, the 26th over the 23rd to the 19th and work over it 2 buttonhole loops with each strand, then with the 8 strands which have *not* been used as foundations 1 raised spot, then the last strand used as a foundation over the next 5, and work 2 buttonhole loops over it with each strand, then the corresponding strand is placed over the next 5, and 2 buttonhole loops worked with each strand, then a similar knotted row, and, lastly, a similar row with the corresponding strand on the other side, which completes the medallion. Continue the pattern of the medallion, and repeat from *. The following rows, as may be seen from the illustration, are the same as the medallion patterns and the first rows of the border. The pattern inside the squares formed by the medallions is only rows of double knots in reversed position with a medallion in the centre. The row of purls round the border is worked as follows:—* 6 buttonhole knots with the first of 8 strands over the 2nd with 1 purl between the 2nd and 3rd and 4th and 5th. The purls are made by working the buttonhole stitch a little way off the preceding and then pushing it close up, then 2½ double knots with the 3rd and 8th strand over the intervening ones, then these 6 strands placed by the one used before as a foundation and 6 buttonhole knots worked over them with 1 purl before the 1st and between the 2nd and 3rd and 4th and 5th; these knots must be tied very tight, so that the foundation does not seem too thick. Lastly, turn back the 8 strands on the wrong side of the work and cut off the projecting strands.

Nos. 387 and 388. Work-Bag (Macramé Work). Dark red plush bag, lined with silk of the same colour, hemmed and drawn up with a silk cord of the same colour. The macramé trimming is knotted from the pattern given in No. 388 with écru-coloured purse silk. Fold in half 162 strands of silk about 2 yards long and knot and knot them to a double foundation thread tied

361

Macramé Lace.

in a circle. 1st round: 1 double knot with every 4 strands. 2nd round: A double foundation thread is laid across the strands, close under the knots, 2 buttonhole knots with every strand in succession over the foundation thread. 3rd round: 1 double knot with every 8 strands, using the centre 4 as a foundation. 4th round: 8 half double knots with the last 4 of one pattern and the first 4 of the next, using the centre 4 of these 8 strands as a foundation. 5th and 6th rounds: Like the 3rd and 2nd. 7th round: Every pattern requires 18 strands. * Twice alternately place the 1st strand across the 2nd to the 9th and work over it 2 buttonhole knots with each strand

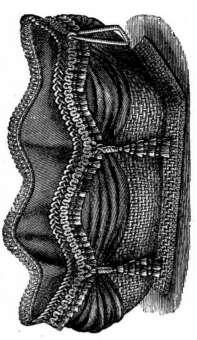

399.—BASKET FOR LAYETTE.

in succession, then work a similar pattern, but in reversed position, with the 10th to the 17th, then 1 double knot with the centre 4 of the 18 strands; repeat from *. 8th round: 1 double knot with every 3 strands, using only 1 strand as a foundation. 9th round: Like the 7th. 10th round: 3 double knots with the last 9 of 1 pattern and the first 9 of the next, using the centre 16 as a foundation. 11th to 13th rounds: Like the 7th to the 9th. 14th round: Every pattern requires 36 strands, and takes in the last 9 of the 1st pattern and the first 9 of the next but one; * 1 double knot with the 7th, 8th,

362

Fringe for Layette.

9th, 10th, 11th, and 12th strands, and with the 25th, 26th, 27th, 28th, 29th, and 30th, using the centre 4 as a foundation, then

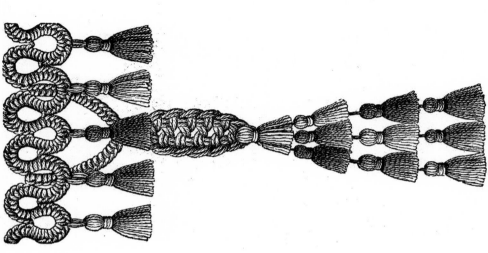

400.—DETAIL OF 399.

863

1 double knot with the 4th, 5th, 6th, 7th, 8th, and 9th, the 10th to the 15th, the 22nd to the 27th, and the 28th to the 33rd, using 2 strands as a foundation, then 6 times 1 double knot

Macramé Lace.

with the next 6 of the same 36 strands, using 4 strands as a foundation; repeat from *. 15th round: * 5 separate double knots with the centre 30 of the 36 strands, using 2 strands as a foundation, then 4 separate double knots with the centre 24,

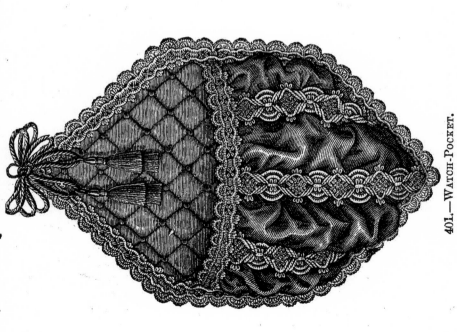

401.—WATCH-POCKET.

864

using 4 as a foundation, then 3 separate double knots with the centre 18, using 2 as a foundation, then 2 separate double knots with centre 12 strands, using 4 as a foundation, then 1 double knot with centre 6 strands, using 2 as a foundation; repeat from *. 16th round: For the outline of every vandyke * place

[25]

Macramé Lace.

Then knot the remaining strands to form the fringe as shown in the illustration, adding fresh strands when necessary.

Nos. 390 and 392. Towel. (Cross Stitch, Holbein and Knotted Stitch.) Towel of coarse white linen, with an embroidered border and knotted fringe at each end. When the pattern is worked, the towel is hemmed at each end, and the fringe is knotted with coarse white thread as follows. (No. 392.) A number of strands of about 24 inches long are folded in half, and knotted together two and two, by making a knot with the 2nd and 3rd strand over the 1st and 2nd, and then with the 1st and 2nd over the 2nd and 3rd. (See No. 392, which represents a pattern of the fringe in the original size.) The knots are then fastened to the weight cushion with pins in a straight line. Close underneath the knots arrange a double foundation thread, and work the 1st row from left to right as follows : 2 buttonhole knots, with each strand over the foundation thread. 2nd row : Like the preceding, but consulting the illustration, and tying together every 8 strands, by taking the 5th and 6th under the 4th and 3rd and over the 1st and 2nd, then the 7th and 8th over the 4th and 3rd and under the 1st and 2nd. 3rd row : Each pattern takes 32 strands, and the spaces must be measured from the illustrations, the strands being numbered according to the order in which they come in the work. * Knot the centre 8 of the 32 strands in the manner we described above, and then twice alternately carry the 9th end aslant across the 10th to the 16th, and work over it 2 buttonhole loops in succession with each strand, then work a similar pattern in reversed direction with the 17th to the 24th strands, then 2 buttonhole loops with the 16th over the 17th strand, plait the 9th to the 16th strands as above described, twice alternately carry one strand over the 2nd to the 16th, and work over it 2 buttonhole loops with each in succession, then work a similar pattern in reverse position with the 17th to the 32nd, repeat from *. 4th row : With every 4 strands, twice alternately 1 buttonhole loop with the 1st

366

Details of Watch-Pocket.

the last 2 strands of one pattern over the first of the next, and work over them 2 buttonhole loops with each of the 6 in succession, then place the 3rd and 4th strand over the 5th and 6th, and work with the latter 2 buttonhole knots in succession, 2 buttonhole knots with the first foundation strands, and with the 7th to the 9th over 3rd and 4th, then place the 8th and 9th strands over the 10th to the 12th, and work 2 buttonhole knots

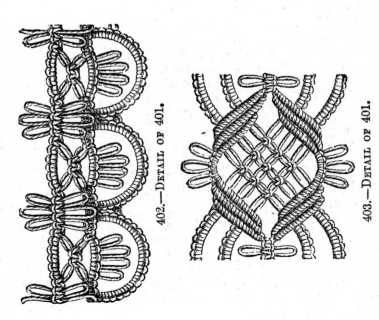

402.—Detail of 401.

403.—Detail of 401.

365

with them and with the former foundation strands, and with the next 3 strands over the 8th and 9th, and so on to the end of the vandyke. The other half of the outline is worked in the same pattern, but in reverse order, as shown in No. 388. 1 double knot is worked with the centre 6 strands at the end of each vandyke, using 4 strands as a foundation; repeat from *.

[26]

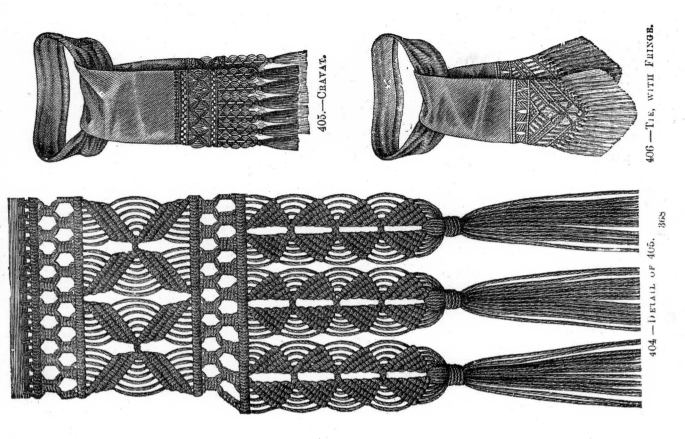

Macramé Lace.

405.—CRAVAT.

406.—TIE, WITH FRINGE.

404.—DETAIL OF 405.   363

Towel.

and 2nd together, over the 3rd and 4th, and then with the latter over the former. 5th row : * Twice alternately carry the 1st end aslant over the 2nd to the 32nd, and tie with each in succession 2 buttonhole knots over it, then a similar pattern with the 17th to the 32nd, then with the 13th to the 16th, and the 17th to the 20th, work a row like the 4th row, but 3 instead of 4 double knots, then with the same 8 strands, 2 double knots with the 1st, 2nd, 7th, and 8th over the rest, but after the first double knot, take in 5 new strands, and tie them to the foundation thread and round the last double knot, then double knot with the last 12 of one pattern and the first 12 of the next, using the centre 8 as a foundation, then knot together the 1st, 2nd, 11th, and 12th on the wrong side, cut the strands even, and wind them lightly round a fine knitting-needle to make them curl.

Nos. 391, 393—396. Towel (Embroidery and Macramé Work). Coarse holland towel, embroidered with coloured cotton and white thread, and finished off at each end with knotted fringe. Trace the design upon the holland, and embroider the design as shown in Nos. 393 to 395 in chain, overcast, feather, knotted, and buttonhole stitch, filling up the figures in herring-bone, plain, and lace stitch.   The outlines are worked with cotton, and the filling up put in with white thread.   When the embroidery is finished, unravel about 4 inches of the holland at each end for the fringe, and knot it as follows :—1st row : Place a double foundation thread across the strands, and tie over it 2 buttonhole knots with each strand in succession.   2nd row : 3 buttonhole knots with every 4th strand over the preceding 3 strands.   3rd row : Like the 2nd row, but in reversed position. 4th row : Like the 1st row.   5th row : 1 double knot with every 4 strands.   6th row : Leave the first 2 strands unnoticed. * 4 double knots with the 1st to the 4th of the first 12 strands, 1 double knot with the 5th to the 8th, 1 double knot with the 9th to the 12th, 1 double knot with the 7th to the 10th, 1 double knot with the 5th to the 8th, 1 double knot with the 9th

367

[27]

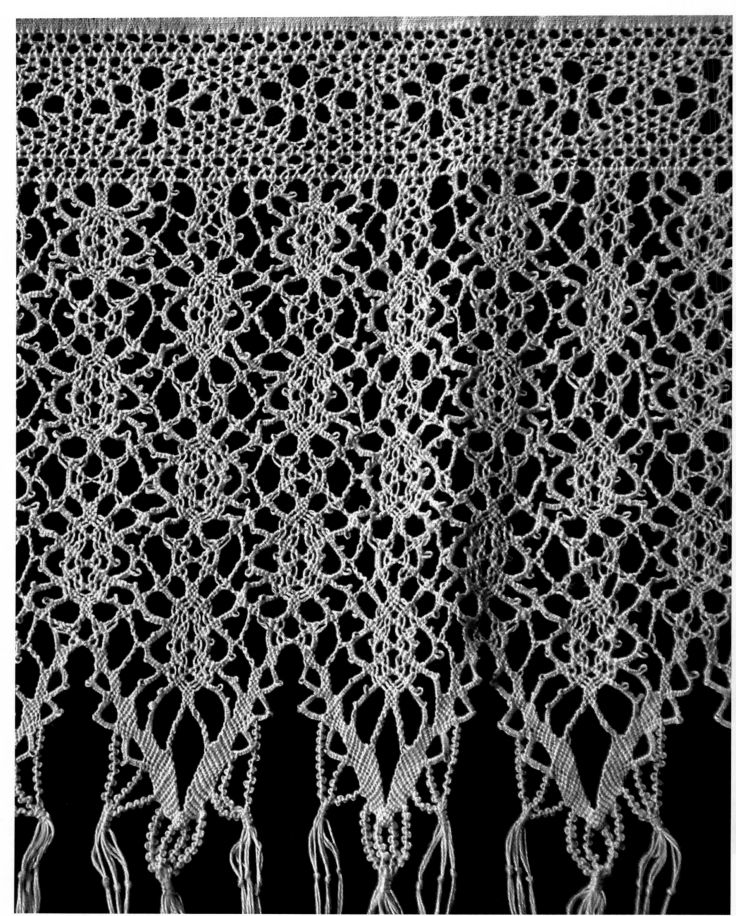

MACRAME TOWEL FRINGE, 19TH C.
from collection of LACIS MUSEUM OF LACE AND TEXTILES [JGG.14751]

THE YOUNG LADIES' JOURNAL

COMPLETE GUIDE TO THE WORK-TABLE.

NO. 12.—KNOTTING OR MACRAMÉ.

FRINGE IN TWO COLOURS.

KNOTTING OR MACRAMÉ.

No. 12 SUPPLEMENT, GRATIS WITH THE APRIL PART, 1883.

DESCRIPTION OF ILLUSTRATION ON FIRST PAGE.

FRINGE OF TWO COLOURS.

This fringe is worked with twenty-four strands of one colour, and eight of the other. They are put over a single leading bar, and knotted as shown in No. 4. A second bar is then laid on close to the first, and the strands are worked closely over it (see No. 5, in progress and finished). The slanting bars are shown in progress in Nos. 7 and 8. They are arranged to form a square at the top, and two bars worked closely with spaces, alternating for six times, then the second square.

The work must be continued row by row. After beginning with the square of bars of the dark colour work a line of six Solomon knots with the light colour, then a second square of bars with the dark, continue for the length of the cushion.

For the second and following lines work the bars over the first and second outer strands of the light colour, and then five Solomon knots with the light colour. In this row the light colour is worked once between the bars.

After this explanation we think it will be easier to work from the design than from description. The raised circular balls, forming the diamond in the centre of the bar diamond, are worked with four Solomon knots, after finishing which, take the two centre strands, pass them together between the second and third strands at the top of the knot, and draw them down at the back, and work one Solomon knot; when the heading is worked the threads must be strongly tied together at the bottom, to form a loop in which to pass the tassel strands through, which are afterwards bound round with a needle and thread; the thread is wound evenly round five or six times, and the needle is passed from the top to the bottom to fasten it.

KNOTTING OR MACRAMÉ.

Knotting or macramé work has recently revived in interest, therefore we repeat our elementary directions which were produced some years since, but have long been out of print. To those directions we add very considerably, in order to make the working of the various designs as simple to our readers as they can be made.

The origin of knotting is very remote. A book of designs was printed in Venice as long ago as 1530; it was then known as *punto a gruppo*, or *gruppino*. In Italy it was used for trimming priests' vestments. The name macramé was given to the work by the Genoese, who employed it for trimming bridal-dresses. The word macramé comes from an Arabian word which signifies a large serviette or cloth, which had a fringed border. Our English name knotting is the more correct one, as the work is formed entirely by knots in varied groupings.

TOOLS REQUIRED:

The lead cushion is the first thing. Our design shows a German cushion for the purpose; we, however, prefer to use one without a handle. The cushion may be fitted into a box. The box should be 15 inches long and 4 inches in height, and 5 inches in width; it should have a lead weight running the entire length not less than ¾ inch in thickness. The box can be covered with Berlin work or an embroidered band. The lead must be enclosed by a cushion filled with bran, and covered with a piece of satin or velvet, or even better, a piece of good, finely-striped ticking. The covering should be a fast colour, so that the dye does not come off to soil the work. The cushion should be fully 2 inches above the wooden box, in order that the leaders may be easily fixed to it. If it is not easy to get lead for the cushion to fill it with sand is the next best thing.

GLASS-HEADED PINS.

Two sizes of these pins may be procured for knotting. They are very convenient to use, as the large heads prevent the loops from slipping.

STEEL CROCHET HOOKS.

The crochet hook is often very convenient for drawing the knots through; these must be chosen of a size to suit the material to be worked with. A sharp pair of scissors will be found needful for cutting the lengths evenly.

MATERIALS.

Macramé cords are now to be had in several sizes both in plain and mixed colours. Crochet cotton, linen thread, silk twist or cord, and gold and silver thread, are all suitable materials for knotting, and make more or less elegant fringes, laces, insertions, and headings for trimming articles of dress, furniture, and fancy-work. Knotting can be worked into linen, &c., by drawing the threads intended to be made into lace or fringe through the material, and looping once; the material can then be fixed to the lead cushion, and the threads knotted. Java canvas and crash, or strong Irish linen or huckaback, may be ornamented with knotting by drawing the threads one way out, and leaving the others to be knotted.

GENERAL HINTS.

The great beauty of knotting rests in the evenness of the work, and as no tracing or outline of any kind can be used, clever manipulation is needed and correct distances must be kept; these can only be mea-

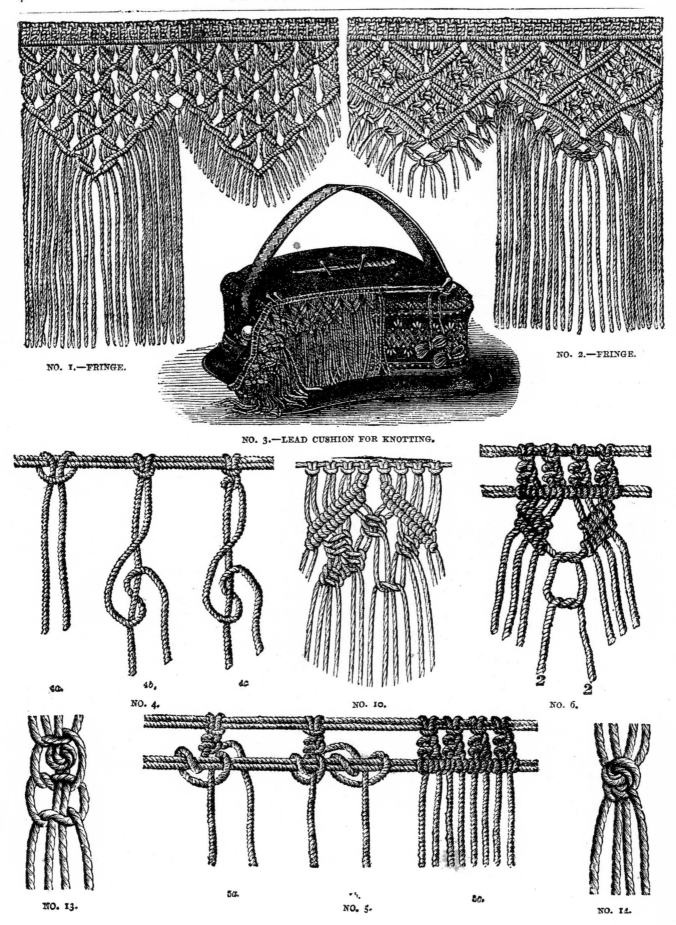

NO. 1.—FRINGE.

NO. 2.—FRINGE.

NO. 3.—LEAD CUSHION FOR KNOTTING.

NO. 4.

NO. 10.

NO. 6.

NO. 13.

NO. 5.

NO. 14.

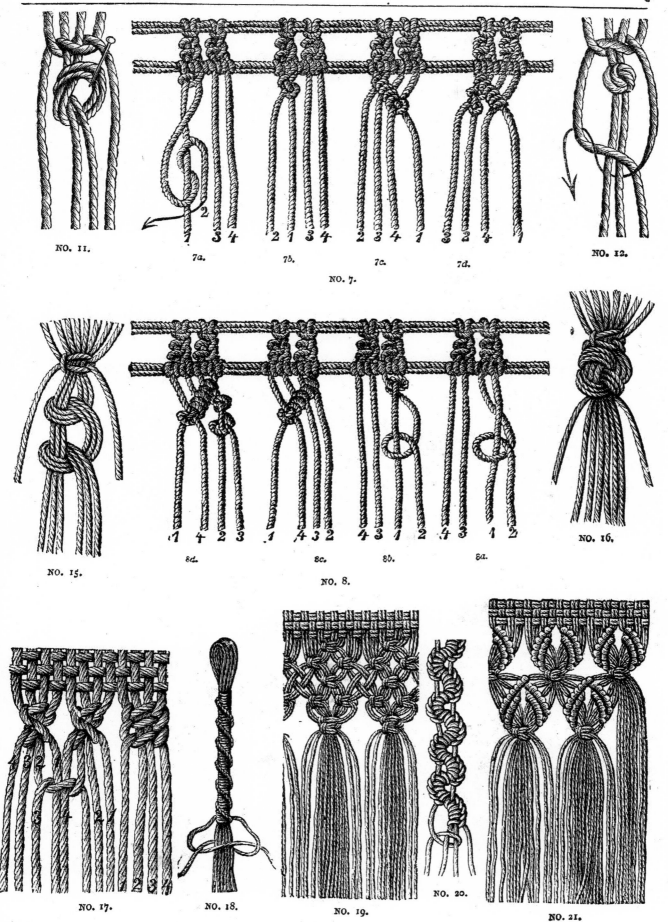

NO. 11.

7a.   7b.   7c.   7d.

NO. 7.

NO. 12.

NO. 15.

8d.   8c.   8b.   8a.

NO. 8.

NO. 16.

NO. 17.   NO. 18.   NO. 19.   NO. 20.   NO. 21.

sured by the eye, added to which you must be quite certain to keep the threads in the order they are at first looped on so as not to twist or turn them. Beginners must before trying patterns practise the varied knots which form them, and be sure that they can tie them firmly and evenly. Try a pattern previous to working it, measure the length of the strands needed to form it, and cut your strands into the lengths required before beginning the work.

No. 1.—FRINGE.

After learning the mode of laying on the heading, working the macramé knot and slanting ribs, this fringe may be attempted as it is but a simple pattern; threads about a yard long will be needed for it, and the entire mode of working each detail is clearly given in Nos. 4 to 9. We abstain from further description, knowing that with the assistance of continued reference to the diagrams the work is more likely to be correctly done than it could be from description.

No. 2.—FRINGE.

The heading is like that shown finished at the end of No. 5. The slanting ribs are the same as those shown in Nos. 6 to 8, but are worked with eight instead of four strands; the double Solomon knots are worked in the same way as shown in No. 10, but with four instead of eight Solomon knots.

No. 3.—LEAD CUSHION FOR KNOTTING.

The mode of making the cushion is described under tools used for knotting. We now call attention to the mode of laying on the threads or bar used for the foundation. The work on the cushion is No. 1 Fringe in progress. Observe the mode of placing the pins and of winding the strands into loops for continuation of heading bar, when the length on the cushion is finished. The foundation lines are also known as cross bars and leaders.

No. 4.—LEADING-BAR WITH THREADS LAID ON AND MACRAME KNOT.

No. 4 shows the manner of fastening on the threads, which should be done with a crochet-hook. Take the loop in the middle and hold it before the bar, pass the two ends upwards behind the bar, bring them down over it, and under the loop draw up tightly (see 4a). The two loops—which, one after the other, are knotted with the threads on the right; round the thread on the left hand only—must be worked with the first loop knot for the beginning (see 4b, and for the finished knot see 4c).

No. 5.—BAR WITH KNOTS.

No. 5 shows the knots in progress, also finished heading and the mode of laying on and working over a second leader-line or cross-bar. 5a and 5b show knots worked over the under cross-threads, which are now laid on, and knots on knots, as described in No. 4, placed in a line complete the heading of the trimming, as shown in No 5c.

No. 6.—HEADING WITH SLANTING RIBS.

The knots in No. 6 follow closely upon each other, forming slanting ribs, which are turned in two opposite directions, and are worked to form double and treble slanting ribs.

The separate looping of the ribs of knots resemble each other exactly. In working from the right towards the left the knotting thread is looped from underneath round the thread laid on; whilst in going from the left towards the right, the loop is formed by placing the knotting thread over the thread laid on.

To make the rib, always make a complete double knot round the outermost of the threads laid on with each of the remaining threads.

Great care must always be taken to hold the thread that is laid on firmly with the left hand, whilst the right makes the loops round it.

No. 6 also shows the cross-knot which completes the slanting rib (see 2-2).

No. 7.—SLANTING RIB IN PROGRESS FROM LEFT TO RIGHT.

No. 7 shows the number of threads, their position and gradual working. Follow 7a for the working of first slanting rib. 7b shows the changed position of the threads after working the first knot of rib; 7c shows the first slanting rib finished, and the position of threads after the first knot of second rib.

No. 8. — SLANTING RIB IN PROGRESS FROM RIGHT TO LEFT.

Now the worker must give attention to 8a, which shows the first looping and position of threads after it; 8b shows the first looping and making of the first knot; 8c a finished rib; 8d second rib in progress. No amount of directions that we can give could by any possibility be so clear to the reader as these numbered positions of the threads.

It is generally considered that it is easier to learn to make the knotted ribs from the right towards the left, as it is the more natural way of working.

No. 9. — HEADING - RIBS AND DIAMONDS FINISHED AND IN PROGRESS.

This diagram will materially assist the worker in executing fringe No. 1, as it is here shown in an increased size with the scallops in progress. Observe the length of threads left to form diamonds between the slanting ribs, also the knots finishing the diamonds before beginning two other slanting ribs.

No. 10.—RIBS WITH EIGHT STRANDS AND DIAMOND CENTRE, WITH TRIANGLE SIDE FORMED OF SOLOMON KNOTS.

Nos. 11, 12, 13, and 14.—SPHERICAL KNOT.

The spherical knot placed singly or in triangles, and diamonds between slanting ribs, gives a rich heading to a fringe. It is begun with a flat Solomon knot, for which four strands are needed, the two centre strands hang straight, the right-hand thread is crossed horizontally over the two centre strands and under the left-hand strand. The left thread is crossed under the two centre strands and over the right-hand strand. The two centre strands are now drawn through to form the centre of spherical knot, and a pin is passed through the knot into the cushion (see No. 11). To complete the knot (see No. 12) pass the left-hand thread over the two centre strands and under the right strand, and the right-hand strand under the two centre strands and over the left-hand strand; draw up. No. 13 shows a spherical knot with two Solomon knots worked under; No. 14 shows it with but one above and below.

The irregular placing of the diagrams is unavoidable because we are obliged to keep our Work-table Guide Supplements to one size on account of binding them.

Nos. 15, 16, AND 24.—RICH KNOT WORKED WITH EIGHT STRANDS.

This knot is composed of a Solomon knot at the top and bottom of two single chain together, worked with six strands.

No. 17.—CROSS KNOT FOR OPEN DIAMONDS.

This knot will only show well in coarse materials. Begin with two Solomon knots, as shown on the right-hand side; the centre and left strands show two finished cross knots, and the figures the mode of dividing the strands to form open diamonds. After working the two Solomon knots cross the right-hand thread under the two centre threads. The left-hand thread over the three strands, then pass it at the back through to the front between the top of the first and second strands, and work the right-hand thread in the same way through the top of third and fourth strands. Now cross the outer strands, slanting over the front of the knot, and pass them through the loop below the knot on each side. Begin again as shown in lower part of diagram.

No. 18.—SPIRAL CORD.

This cord can be made with any required number of centre strands, and is always worked with the two outer side strands. Take the right-hand strand, pass it behind the centre strands and over the left-hand strand; take the left-hand strand and put it over the centre strands and under the right-hand strand, draw tight and repeat.

No. 19.—FRINGE, WITH DOUBLE KNOT HEADING.

Double loops are taken as described for the beginning of No. 17, and are formed into the open knot by working Solomon knots with two threads taken from each side alternately. This heading may be made of whatever depth you please.

No. 20.—WAVED BAR.

This bar is formed of four strands; five singles are knotted over two strands in succession with the left-hand thread, then five singles with the right-hand thread alternately.

No. 21.—FRINGE FOR JAVA CANVAS.

Take eight threads, work two slanting ribs of six knots each; cross all the threads with a Solomon knot worked with two threads of the canvas. Be careful to observe the correct distances, and work the second line of pattern alternating the threads.

Nos. 22 AND 23.—PICOT HEADING.

The first diagram shows the mode of pinning on strands to form a picot heading. Two strands are fastened by a pin to the cushion; two or more Solomon-knots are worked according to the height of the heading. No. 23 shows picot heading with the leading bar laid on, and the threads of the picots knotted round it.

No. 24.—See No. 15.

No. 25.—WAVED LOOP.

The loop is composed of four strands, and three macramé knots worked with three strands; the right-hand strand is left hanging until the third knot is worked, when it is used with the other three strands to form the Solomon knot closing the groups.

No. 26.—SIMPLE CHAIN.

Begin with a Solomon knot with the two centre threads; work with the right-hand thread a single chain over the left, then with the left-hand thread a single chain over the right. This is sometimes used in fringes.

No. 27.—LEADING BAR WORKED OVER WITH SOLOMON KNOTS.

Two strands of the length for the work must be pinned through the middle for the bar, two working threads are required which must be three times the length of bar, with these cover the bar with Solomon knots, then draw strands through each of two loops, pass over two and repeat, work each group with four Solomon knots.

Nos. 28 AND 30.—KNOTTED HEADING OF FRINGED THREADS.

This is useful for serviette, dinner-waggon cloths, &c. Separate the threads in six strands, pass the second right-hand strand round the left and draw it out between the two. The second tie is like the first part of a Solomon's knot, tie the third and fourth strand as described for the first and second, alternate the strands and tie in the same way in the second and following rows.

No. 29.—FRINGE FOR KNITTED COUNTER-PANES, &c.

The edge of the counterpane is shown, through this the loops to work the strands into, must be drawn, passing over two stitches of the knitting draw up a single knot and leave the loop the length shown in the design, draw through every loop with double strands fastened as described in No. 4. In every fourth loop draw through a double strand without knotting it (see design). Observe, two strands of this group are left unworked; work a row of two Solomon knots together with two alternate strands from each cluster. In the next row two clusters of two Solomon knots, and in the third one Solomon knot to finish the scallop, twenty strands are knotted together once for the fringe.

No. 30.—See No. 28.

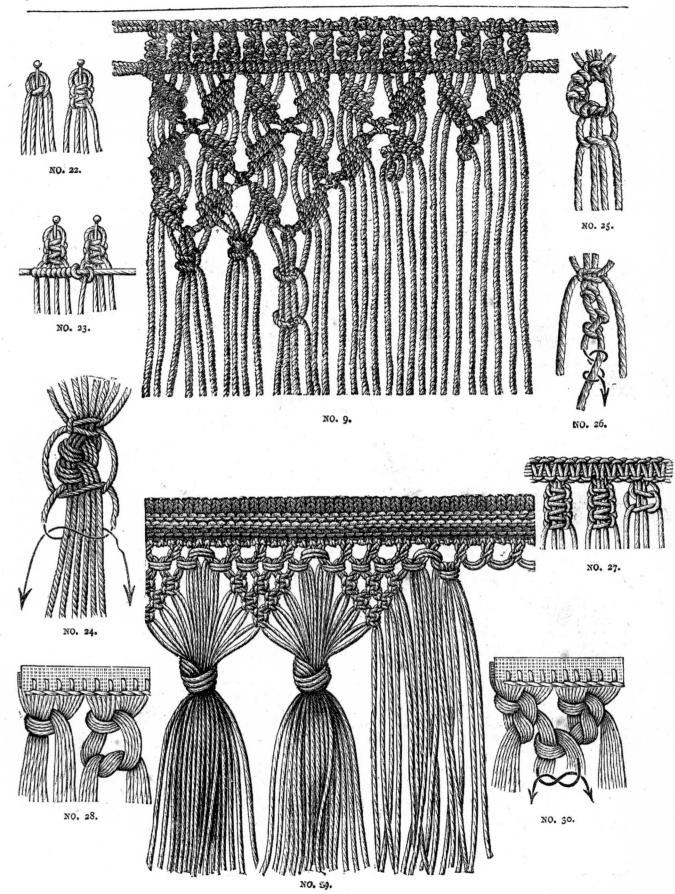

NO. 22.

NO. 23.

NO. 24.

NO. 28.

NO. 9.

NO. 29.

NO. 25.

NO. 26.

NO. 27.

NO. 30.

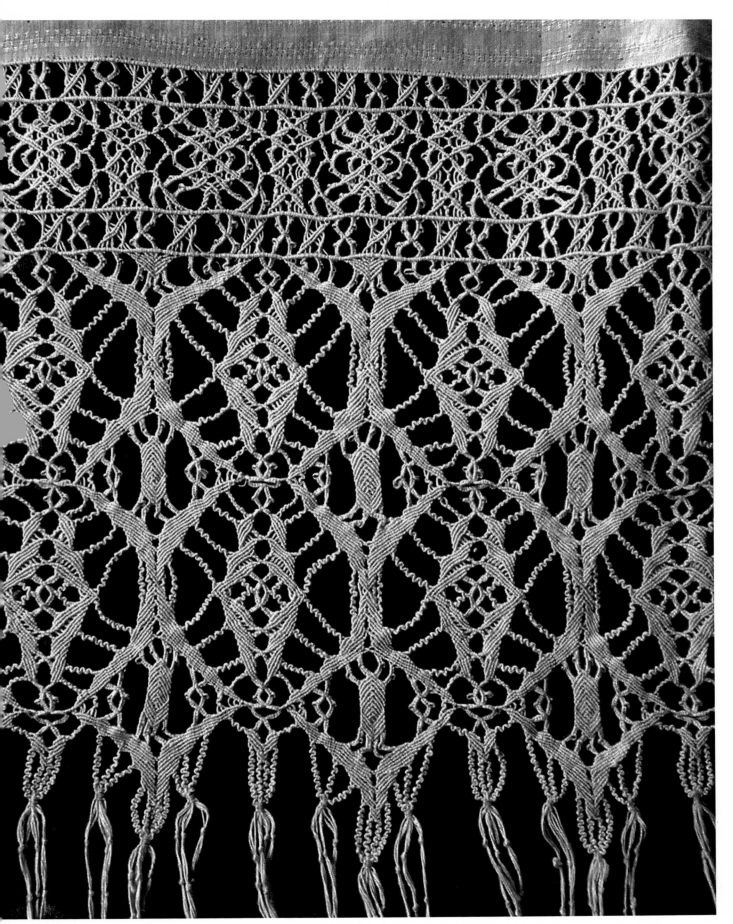

MACRAME TOWEL FRINGE, 19TH C.
from collection of LACIS MUSEUM OF LACE AND TEXTILES [JGG.14749]

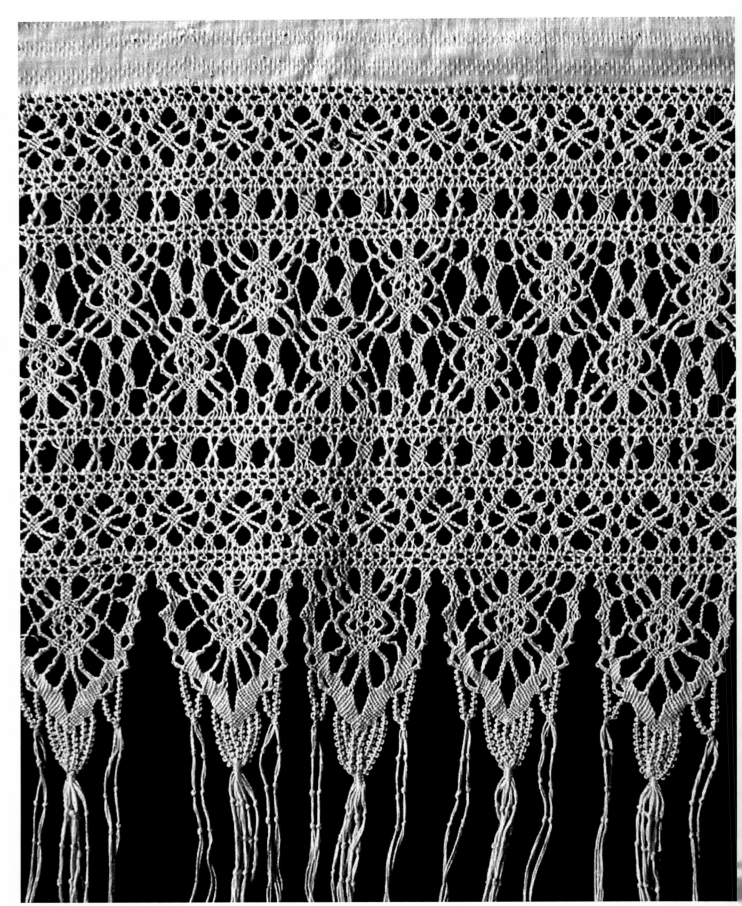

MACRAME TOWEL FRINGE, 19TH C.
from collection of LACIS MUSEUM OF LACE AND TEXTILES [JGG.14741]

THE IMPERIAL
MACRAMÉ LACE BOOK.

WITH NUMEROUS ILLUSTRATIONS AND INSTRUCTIONS.

FLAX THREADS.

BARBOUR BROTHERS,

No. 134 CHURCH STREET, NEW YORK.

SEVENTH EDITION.

THE GRAPHIC COMPANY, PRINTERS, 39-41 PARK PLACE, N. Y.

1881.

INTRODUCTION.

IN introducing this work on Macramé Lace, we are acting in compliance with the wishes of our numerous friends, who are desirous of seeing a fuller developement of this interesting study. The subject of Macramé, so well known in ancient times, is now so much in favor that it has already found its way into the principal Courts of Europe, and we take this method of introducing it to the Ladies of America, beliving they will find it a fascinating yet simple study.

It is remarkable that this knotted Lace, Macramé, in spite of its ancient date, should have been generally unknown in this country, until we had the honor and privilege of introducing it. Its history goes back to a very early date. Knotted threads in the most ingenious and varied designs may be seen in the pattern books of the 16th century.

We have no doubt that as soon as the subject of this beautiful art is understood, it will be taken up and developed by all lovers of Lace work.

BARBOUR BROTHERS.

134 Church Street, New York; 153 Franklin Street, Boston;
511 Market St., San Francisco; 26 Bank Street, Philadelphia.

FLAX THREAD WORKS.

HILDEN MILLS, BARBOUR FLAX SP'G CO.
Lisburn, Ireland. *Paterson, N. J.*

Introduction to Seventh Edition.

It is now a little more than two years since we issued the first Edition of our Illustrated Book of Instructions on Macramé Lace Making. Our aim was to lead the ladies into a channel of beautiful and useful work, which had previously been comparatively unknown in this country.

How well we have succeeded the great and still growing interest in Macramé Lace Making will best attest. Flax threads are best adapted for lace and crotcheting purposes, possessing, as they do, the qualities of strength, durability and a rich silkiness of finish. We shall continue to give special attention to manufacturing full lines of Macramé and other Flax Threads, which the wants and taste of the Ladies may demand.

BARBOUR BROTHERS,

134 *Church Street, New York.*

PATENT MACRAME LACE DESK.

PRICE, $3.00 EACH, COMPLETE.

MATERIALS FOR MACRAMÉ LACE.

An accompanying Cut shows a Patent Lace Desk complete. This is the first requisite. They are made in Blue and Scarlet. Are quite light and can be used either on a table or on the knee. Ladies traveling can readily put one in their trunk as they do not get out of order. The cleats at the side of the desk are for fastening the straight lines of the threads, the swinging bar is for fastening the threads when working, and is to substitute the use of the buttons on a lady's dress which have been generally used for this purpose. The desk is simple, yet complete, and the uses of the several attachments will readily suggest themselves.

Flax threads should only be used which are manufactured specially by Barbour Brothers, in all sizes for Macramé Lace. They are put up in large hanks, and two pounds in a red box. Sold by the principal Wholesale and Retail Fancy Goods Stores in America.

Instructions for Making Macramé Lace.

THE straight lines may be cut the length of the lace required, and should always be double threads; but if cut too short for the purpose, fresh threads may be joined to those, by tying them together with a weaver's knot. The flax threads for working should be cut to the exact size given with each pattern; but when the required length is not known, cut the threads a good bit longer than is necessary, and work out one scollop. Then measure how much the fringe is deeper than required, and cut the next threads shorter by so much. The heavier threads are used in making the lace, when intended for lambrequins, mantels and furniture trimmings generally, and the finer linen threads of various sizes, for dress trimmings, altar linen, or many other purposes which suggest themselves.

The lace is made by knotting threads together. One thread is held firmly over the other as leader, and each single thread is knotted twice on to it. When a leaf is worked from right to left, the leader is held in the left hand, and when a leaf is worked from left to right, the leader is held in the right hand. Pin on as many straight lines as are required for the pattern.

In commencing a pattern, fasten the threads for working on to the top line as follows:—Pass the two ends of each thread under the line, pointing them up, then draw them back through the loop, repeat to the end of the desk, then put in a pin between every four threads, then loosen the second line, hold it firmly in the right hand, and knot each thread twice on to it with the left hand. The straight lines are always worked in this way. The lace, as a rule, should be worked tightly as it adds much to its beauty and durability.

No. 1.

A.—Single Chain.

Take two threads, hold one straight in the left hand, knot the other thread on to it once with the right hand; hold this thread straight in the right hand and knot the other on to it with the left. **Repeat.**

B.—Double Chain.

This is made in the same way as the single chain, but with four threads, using two threads each time instead of one.

C.—Open Chain.

Take four threads, commence with the two at the left side, hold the first of these in the right hand as leader, knot the second twice on to it with the left hand, pass the same leader to the left hand, knot the same thread as before twice on to it; take the next two threads, hold the first thread in the right hand as leader, knot the second thread twice on to it, pass the leader to the left hand, knot the same thread as before twice on to it, hold the leader still in

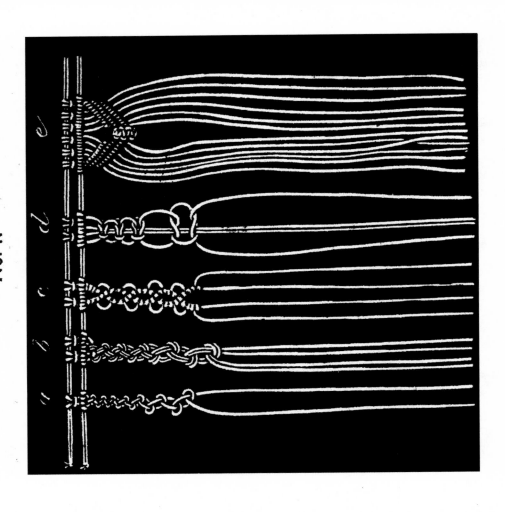

No. I.

the left hand, and knot the first leader twice on to it with the right hand; knot the remaining thread at the left side twice on to it, leaving a loop before drawing it up tight.* Pass the same leader back to the right hand, and knot the same thread twice on to it with the left hand. Then take up the two threads at the right side, hold the under one in the right hand, as leader, knot the other thread twice on to it, leaving a loop as before. Pass the same leader to the left hand, and knot the same thread twice on to it. Hold the leader still in the left hand, and knot the leader at the left side twice on to it; knot the remaining thread at the left side on to it, leaving a loop as before. Then pass the leader back to the right hand, and knot same thread twice on to it. Repeat from* on preceding page.

_____

D.—Solomon's Knot.

Take four threads, hold the two centre ones straight; pass the thread at left side loosely over these. Take the thread at right side, pass it over the first thread and under the centre ones, and up through the loop at left side; draw it up tight. Then take the right-hand thread, pass it over the two centre ones loosely; take the left thread, pass it over this, under the centre ones, and up through the loop at the right side; draw it up tight to meet the first part of the knot. This forms one Solomon's Knot.

_____

* It would be well to observe that, in making this open chain, after the loops are made, the leader is always passed into the other hand, and the thread knotted twice on to it.

E.—Raised Picot.

The Raised Picot mostly comes between two leaves. Take the four centre threads—two from each leaf—hold the two centre ones straight and make six Solomon's knots on to them ; pass the two centre threads down through the opening between the two leaves ; take one of these threads and knot it once to the thread at the left side, take up the other and knot it once to the remaining thread at the *right side*.

No. 2.

(Threads for this Pattern one yard and two inches long.)

Pin on the straight lines in the usual way, then fasten on the threads to the top line, after which loosen the second line, and knot each thread twice on to it with the left hand. Make a row of Solomon's knots thus : —Take four threads, hold the two centre ones straight, pass the thread at the left side over them loosely, then pass the thread at the right side over this, under the two centre ones, and up through the loop at the left side ; draw it up tight. Then pass the right thread over the two centre ones, pass the left thread over this, under the two centre ones, and up through the loop at the right side, draw it up tight to meet the first part of the knot. Repeat to the end of desk. Then loosen the third line, hold in the right hand, and knot each thread twice on to it with the left.

First Oval.—*Take eight threads ; divide them into two parts. Begin by holding the fourth thread in the left hand as leader, and knot each of the three threads twice on to it with the right ; then take the next four threads, hold the first of these in the right hand as leader and knot the three threads on to it with the left hand, then take the two

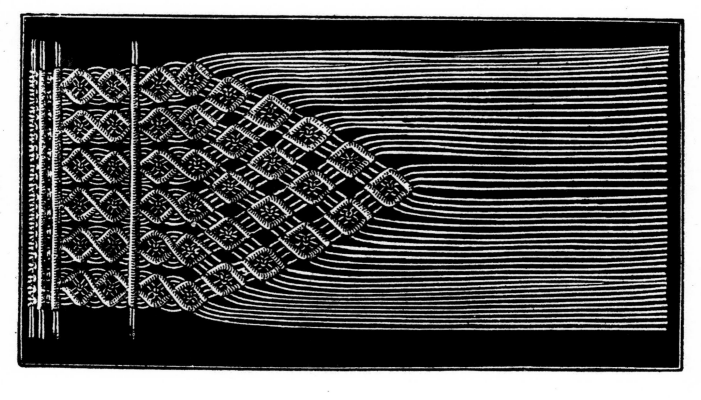

No. 2.

No. 3.

(Threads for this Pattern one yard three inches long.)

Pin on the straight lines in the usual way, after which fasten on the threads thus: Pass the two ends of each thread under the top line, pointing them up, then bring them through the loop, then loosen the second line, hold it in the right hand, and knot each thread twice on to it with the left hand. Then take two threads; hold the first in the left hand, knot the other three times on to it with the right hand; repeat this to the end of the desk. Then take one thread from each; hold one in the right hand, and knot the other on to it with the left hand; repeat to the end of desk. Then loosen the third line at the right side, hold it in the right hand, and knot each thread twice on to it with the left hand, *Take the first six threads, hold the first thread in the right hand as leader, knot the five threads on to it with the left hand, each thread twice; then make the second row of the leaf thus:—Hold the first thread at the left side again in the right hand, knot each of the five threads twice on to it with the left hand; then take the next six threads, hold the sixth thread in the left hand as leader, and knot each of the five threads twice on to it with the right hand; then make the second row of the leaf by holding the sixth thread again in the left hand and knotting each of the five threads on to it with the right; then hold the same thread as leader in the left hand, and knot the leader of the first leaf twice on to it; then make the third leaf, hold the same leader still in the left hand, and knot the threads on to it with the right hand; then take the six threads and repeat for a second line; then take the six threads at the right side, hold the first of these (that is the left side one) in the right hand and make the fourth leaf, knotting the threads on with

centre threads from each side and make a Solomon's knot; then tak... the first leader, hold it in the right hand, and knot the three threads ... to it; then take the second leader, hold it in the left hand, and knot t... seven threads on to it with the right hand. Then divide the eig... threads, take the four at the right side, hold the first (at the left side) ... the right hand, knot the three threads on to it with the left hand; the... take the two centre threads from each side and make a Solomon's kno... then take the leader at the right side, hold it in the left hand, knot thr... threads on to it; then take the leader at the right side, hold it in the rig... hand, and knot the remaining three threads on to it with the left han... Repeat from * to the end of desk. Then loosen the fourth line, hold ... in the right hand and knot each thread twice on to it with the left han... Repeat this to the end of the desk; and for the scollop, take eig... threads and repeat from * six times. Then take the top leader from t... second oval, hold it in the left hand, and knot the four threads of th... first oval on to it with the right hand; then take the top thread at th... left side, hold it in the right hand, and knot the three threads of th... second oval on to it. Then make a Solomon's knot in the middle wit... the four centre threads; then take the leader at the left side, hold it i... the right hand, and knot three threads on to it with the left; then tak... the leader at the right side, hold it in the left hand, and knot the fou... threads on to it with the right. Repeat until there are five small oval... then make four under these in the same way, and three under the fou... —and so on—to form the scollop, until it comes to one. If preferre... the fringe may then be knotted, which gives it a rich effect.—See No. ... Pattern.

the left hand ; repeat for the second line : repeat from * to the end of the desk ; then loosen the fourth line, and knot each thread twice on to it in the usual way.

*For the Scollop.—Take eight threads, divide them into two parts ; take the first four threads, hold the first thread in the right hand, and knot the three threads on to it with the left hand. *Second row of Leaf.*—Take the first thread again, hold it in the right hand and knot the three threads on with the left hand ; then take the next four threads, hold the fourth thread as leader in the left hand, and knot each of the three threads on to it with the right. Make the second row of the leaf in the same way ; hold the leader still in the left hand, and join the two leaves by knotting the leader of the first leaf twice on to it. Repeat from * six times, then reduce it one in each row until the point is formed. according to the engraving ; then join the two leaders of the leaves at the point ; then take the first thread at the left side, hold it in the right hand as leader, and knot each thread three times on to it down the side of the scollop to form a continuous line ; then take the thread at right side of the scollop, hold it in the left hand, and knot each thread three times on to it with the right hand ; then join the two leaders by holding one tight and knotting the other twice on to it ; then take the first thread again at the right side, hold it in the left hand and make a second line ; repeat at each side to form a third line. The leader is always held at the top, and the threads underneath, after which the threads are all held back, fastened down with needle and thread on the wrong side, and then cut close.

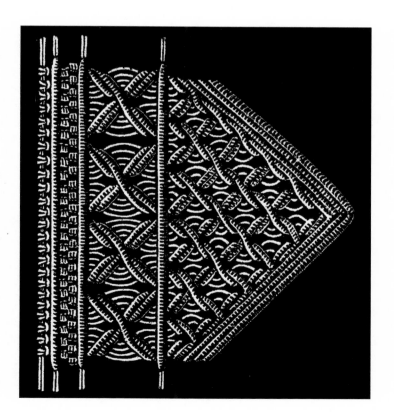

No. 3.

14

No. 4.

(Threads for this Pattern to be one yard long.)

No. 4.

Commence by pinning on the straight lines in the usual way, after which fasten on the threads for working, to the top or first line. Pass the two ends of each thread under the line, pointing them up, then draw them through the loop; then loosen the second line at the right side, and knot each thread twice on to it with the left hand. Then make a row of Solomon's knots with every four threads to the end, after which loosen the third line, and knot the threads on to it as before. Then take four threads and make three Solomon's knots with them. Repeat to the end of the desk. Then loosen the fourth line, and knot each thread twice on to it with the left hand, as before; then take the first four threads, hold the first of these in the right hand as leader, at the top, and knot the three threads on to it with the left (each thread twice): then pass the same leader to the left hand, and knot each of the three threads on to it with the right. Repeat this five times. Then make two more chains, exactly the same as last. Then take six threads; hold the first in the right hand as leader (the leader should always be at top, and the threads underneath), and make a leaf of two rows; then take the next six threads; hold the one at the right side in the left hand as leader, and make a leaf of two rows; then take the two centre threads of each leaf, and with them make a row of six Solomon's knots; then pass the two centre threads of these four between the two leaves, pointing them down, and knot these threads to the other two, to form the raised Picot. Then take the centre thread at the left side, hold it in the left hand as leader, and knot the threads on with the right hand, to make the lower leaf at the left side (two rows); then take the centre thread at the right side, hold it in the

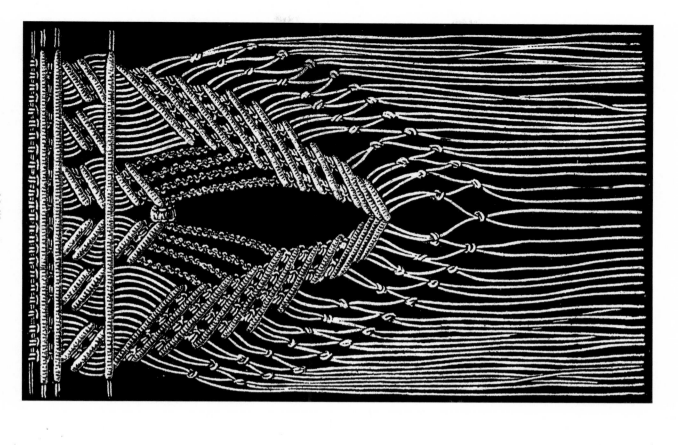

right hand as leader, and make the lower leaf at the right side ; then make three more chains, and then another star of four leaves, with raised Picot in the centre. Repeat to the end of desk. Loosen the fifth line, and knot each thread twice on to it, as before. Take four threads, make three Solomon's knots with these. Repeat to the end of desk. Loosen the sixth line, and knot each thread twice on to it, as before ; then make a row of Solomon's knots with every four threads ; then loosen the seventh line, and knot each thread twice on to it, as before.

To finish off the Insertion.—Keep the last line pinned on at both ends ; take two threads, draw the second one up under the line in a loop, pass the end of both threads through this loop, draw them up tight, to form a knot, same as the one at the top line. The threads will now be in front, between the two last lines. Pass these threads to the back, one at each side of the knot, tie them firmly together at the back ; sew these threads neatly to the work, on the wrong side, with a needle and thread. Repeat to the end of desk, and then cut the threads close.

No 5.

(Threads for this Pattern one yard and four inches long.)

Pin on the straight lines in the usual way, and fasten on the threads for working as described in the former patterns. Loosen the second line, and knot each thread twice on to it to the end of the desk. Take the first four threads, hold three in the right hand,

and knot the first thread twice over them with the left hand; repeat to the end of desk. Loosen the third line, and knot each thread twice on to it as usual. *Take eight threads, hold the first as leader in the right hand, and knot each of the seven threads twice on to it with the left hand; then divide these eight threads into two parts; take the first four of these threads, hold three in the left hand, and knot the fourth thread twice over them with the right hand; do the same to the next four threads; then take the first of these threads, hold it in the right hand, and knot each of the seven threads twice on to it with the left hand. The second and third leaves are made in the same way. *Fourth Leaf.*—Take the eighth thread, hold it as leader in the left hand, and knot each thread twice on to it with the right hand; then divide these eight threads into two parts; take the first four of these threads, hold three in the right hand, and knot the fourth thread twice over them with the left hand. Do the same to the next four threads. Then take the eighth thread again, hold it in the eft hand, and knot each thread on to it with the right hand. Fifth and sixth leaves are made in the same way. Repeat from*. Loosen the fourth line, and knot each thread twice on to it. Commence the scollop. Take sixteen threads, hold the first in the right hand as leader at the top, and the threads underneath, knot each of the fifteen threads twice on to it with the left hand; then divide these sixteen threads into four parts; take the first four threads, hold three in the left hand, and knot the fourth thread twice over them with the right hand; do the same to the other three parts; then take eight threads at centre of scollop, hold the first in the right hand, and knot each of the seven threads twice on to it; divide these eight threads into two parts; take the first four threads, hold three in the left hand, and knot the fourth thread over them twice; do the same to the next four threads; then make a second line with these eight threads; then take

No. 6.

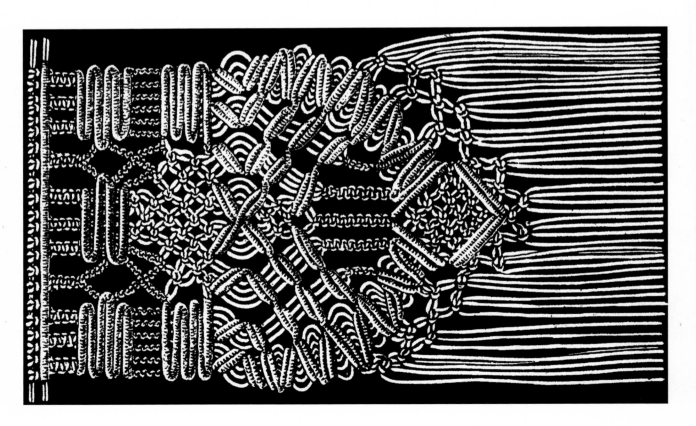

right hand, and knot each thread twice on to it. Take the first four threads, make three Solomon's knots with them; repeat to the end of desk. Take the fourth*row of Solomon's knots, divide the four threads into two parts, make five single chains with the two first threads and eight single chains with the other two threads; then take the eighth row of Solomon's knots, and make six single chains with each two threads. Take the first thread at the left side, hold it in the right hand as leader, and knot eleven threads on to it; then pass the leader to the left hand; and knot the some threads on to it with the right hand; then pass the same leader back to the right hand, and knot the threads on to it with the left, also the two threads of the first single chain. Pass the leader again to the left hand, and knot the threads on to it with the right; pass the leader back to the right hand, and knot the same threads on to it with the left, leaving out the two last threads which are to be knotted in single chain six times, then pass the leader to the left hand, and knot the same threads on to it with the right. Divide these threads into six parts, and make eight single chains with every two threads. Commence at the seventh row of Solomon's knots; take the thread at the right side, hold it in the left hand, and knot eleven threads on to it with the right hand. Divide those twelve threads into six parts, and make two single chains with every two threads. Then pass the thread at the left side to the right hand, and knot each thread twice on to it with the left hand, and also the two threads of the next single chain. Then make another row of single chain. Then pass the same leader back to the left hand, and knot each thread twice on to it, also the threads of the second chain; pass the same leader to the right hand, and knot each thread twice on to it with the left; repeat from * to the end of the desk. Take the two threads at each end of the centre pattern, and make six single chains on each. Make two Solomon's knots with the eight middle threads; make a Solomon's knot

eight more threads, hold the eighth one in the left hand, and knot each of the seven threads into two parts, hold three threads in the right hand, and eight threads into two parts, hold three threads in the right hand, and knot the fourth twice over them with the left hand; do the same to the other four threads. Then make a second line thus—hold the eighth thread in the left hand as leader, and knot the seven threads on to it with the right hand; then take two threads from each side and make six Solomon's knots to form a raised Picot; then take the eight threads at the left side of the scollop, divide them into four parts, and make a single chain with each two threads; the first chain is knotted sixteen times, increase two in each to the centre; then begin at the left side, take up the sixteen threads, leave out two of them, hold the next thread in the right hand as leader, and knot each thread twice on to it; also knot on the two threads of the first single chain on to it; then repeat the knotting up of every four threads, after which make another long line, leaving out the two first threads, and knotting on the two threads of the second chain; repeat this until there are five long rows; then leave out four threads in the two following rows; then make a row with eight threads, and to finish the end of the scollop make four close lines according to the engravings. Repeat for the right hand side of the scollop, holding the leaders in the left hand, and knotting the threads on with the right hand. The last three rows at the end of the scollop are joined together, the threads are then knotted to make a knotted fringe.

No. 6.

(Threads for this Pattern one yard and three quarters long.)

Pin on the straight lines in the usual way, and fasten the threads for working on the top line; then loosen the second line, hold it in the

No. 7.

under these, taking two threads from each knot; make a Solomon's knot at each side, and then one in the centre, and so on, according to the engraving.

And, having clearly described the pattern so far, the rest may be easily copied from the engraving by any worker who has followed the directions to this stage.

The scollop being composed of leaves, with very little variety, the instructions for it would be only a repetition of any of the former patterns.

No. 7.

(Threads for this Pattern one and a half yards long.)

Pin on the lines in the usual way, after which fasten on the threads for working; then loosen the second line, hold it in the right hand, and knot each thread twice on to it with the left. Take four threads, hold the three first ones in the left hand, knot the fourth thread three times over them with the right. Repeat to the end of desk. Take two threads from each, hold three in the right hand and knot the first thread three times over them with the left. Repeat to end of desk. Then loosen the third line, hold it in the right hand, and knot each thread twice over it with the left hand. *Take eight threads, make a Solomon's knot with the first four, hold the eighth thread in the left hand as leader, and knot each thread twice on to it with the right hand, take the eighth thread again as leader, and make a second row same as the last; take the next eight threads, make a Solomon's knot with the last four, then take the

first thread, hold it as leader in the right hand, and knot each of the seven threads twice on to it with the left hand. Then take the eight threads again and make a second row; then make eight Solomon's knots with those threads. After this, take the first thread at the left side, hold it in the right hand as leader, and knot each of the seven threads twice on to it with the left hand. Repeat for a second line. Then take the thread at the right side, hold it in the left hand as leader, and knot each thread twice on to it. Repeat for a second line. Take the first four threads, make a Solomon's knot; the same with last four threads. Then take the next four threads, hold two in each hand, and make twelve double chain; make two more rows of double chain. Repeat from * to the end of desk; Then loosen the fourth line, hold it in the right hand, and knot each thread twice on to it with the left hand. Then take the first four threads, and make a Solomon's knot. Repeat to the end of desk. Loosen the fifth line, hold it in the right hand, and knot each thread twice on to it with the left. *Take six threads, hold the first in the right hand as leader, and knot the five threads on to it with the left. Repeat for two more lines. Take the next six threads, hold the sixth in the left hand, and knot the five threads on to it with the right hand. Repeat for two more lines; then make a raised Picot with the four centre threads; then take the centre thread at the left side, hold it in the left hand, and knot the five threads on to it. Repeat for two more lines. Take the centre thread at the right side, hold it in the right hand, and knot the five threads on to it with the left hand. Repeat for two more lines, then take the next four threads, and make a row of open chains as described in diagram C, then repeat with the next four threads. Repeat from * to the end of desk. Then loosen the sixth line, hold it in the left hand, and knot each thread twice on to it. Take the first four threads, make a Solomon's knot. Repeat to the end of desk ; loosen the seventh line, hold it in the right hand, and knot

[51]

each thread twice on to it. The next part of the insertion is made exactly like the first, and to finish off keep the last line pinned on at both ends, take two threads, draw the second one up under the line in a loop, then pass the ends of both threads through this loop, draw them up tight to form a knot, same as the one on the top line; the two threads will then be in front, between the last two lines, pass these threads to the back, one at each side of the knot, tie the two thready firmly together at the back, sew them neatly down on the wrong side, repeat to the end of desk and cut off the threads close.

No. 8.

(Threads for this Pattern one yard nine inches long.)

Pin on the straight lines or leaders to the desk; then fasten on the threads to the top line, so:—Take a thread; pass the two ends of it under the line, pointing them up, and then bring them down through the loop. Loosen the second leader by taking out the pin at the right side, hold it in the right hand and knot each thread twice on to it with the left hand. Take the first four threads, and with them make three Solomon's knots. (These knots are made as follows: Take four threads, hold the two centre ones straight, pass the thread at the left side loosely over these; then take the thread at the right side, pass it over the first thread, under the centre ones, and up through the loop at the left side; draw it up tight, then take the right hand thread, pass it over the two centre ones loosely; take the left thread, pass it over this, under the centre ones, and up through the loop at the right side, draw it

up tight to meet the first part of the knot). Repeat to the end of the desk. Then loosen the third line by taking out the pin at the right side, hold it in the right hand, and knot each thread twice on to it with the left hand. To make the first leaf:—Take eight threads, hold the first one in the right hand, over the others, and knot each of the seven threads twice on to it with the left hand. Take the first thread again, hold it in the right hand, and knot the threads on to it as before. Take the next eight threads, hold the eighth one in the left hand, and knot each of the seven threads twice on to it with the right hand. Take the eighth thread again, hold it in the right hand, and knot the seven threads on to it as before. Then make a raised Picot, so:—Take the two centre threads of each leaf, and with these four threads make six Solomon's knots; then pass the two centre threads between the two leaves, pointing them down; then knot each of these threads on the two remaining ones, to fasten them; then take the eighth thread, hold it in the left hand, and knot each of the seven threads twice on to it with the right hand; take the eighth thread again, hold it in the left hand, and knot each of the seven threads on to it, as before. Then take the next thread to make the fourth leaf, hold it in the right hand, and knot each of the seven threads twice on to it with the left hand; take up the thread again, hold it in the right hand, and knot each of the seven threads on to it, as before. This forms the first star. Repeat to end of desk. Loosen the fourth line, hold it in the right hand, and knot each thread on to it with the left hand.

The Scollop.

As the scollop is made of these stars, it is not necessary to describe them further; and to finish the scollop, when the stars are all made, take the first thread, hold it in the right hand, and knot each thread twice on to it: but when the stars meet, knot two of the threads three times, instead of twice—this makes the straight line more even, and joins the stars more completely; then take the first thread at the right side of the scollop, hold it in the left hand, and do the same. Repeat at the right side, then at the left side; then take the ninth thread at the left side, hold it in the right hand, and knot the threads on to it with the left hand. Repeat at the right side. Then take the seventeenth thread, hold it in the right hand, and knot the remaining threads on to it with the left hand. Repeat at the right side, to finish the scollop.

No. 9.

(Threads for this Pattern one yard and eighteen inches long.)

Pin on three straight lines, and fasten the threads for working on to the top line in the usual way; then take the pin out of the second line at the right side, hold it in the right hand, and knot each thread twice on to it with the left hand. Repeat with the third line. Take the first four threads, and with them make four Solomon's knot. Repeat to the end of the desk. Then take the first four threads; hold the fourth in the right hand, and knot the first thread of the next four twice on to it; then take the second thread of the second four, hold it in the left hand, and knot two threads of the first four on to it; then take the second thread of the first four, hold it in the right hand, and knot three threads of the second four on to it with the left hand; then take the third thread of the second four, hold it in the left hand, and knot three threads on to the first four on to it; then take the first thread of the first four, hold it in the right hand, and knot the four threads on to it; then take the fourth thread of the second four, hold it in the left hand, and knot the four threads on to it from the other side—this completes the diamond. Repeat to the end of desk.

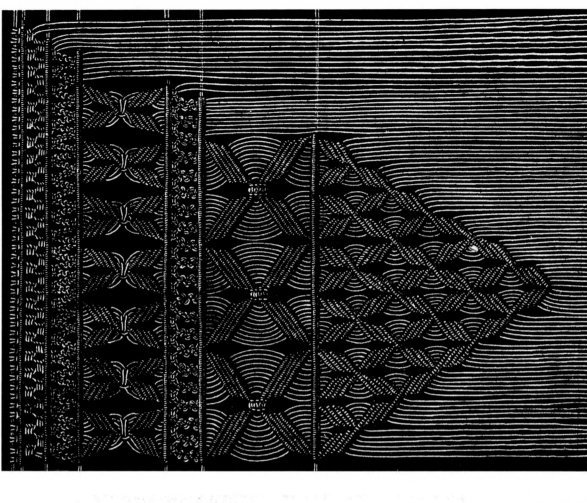

The scollop is formed by leaving out the diamond in each row, until only one diamond remains.

No. 10.

(Threads for this Pattern two yards three inches long.)

Pin on the straight lines or leaders to the desk in the usual way, then fasten the threads for working on to the top line. Loosen the second line at the right side by taking out the pin which confines it to the desk; hold the leader in the right hand, and knot each thread twice on to it with the left; then take the first four threads, hold three in the left hand, and knot the fourth thread three times over them with the right hand. Repeat to the end of desk. Then take the first two threads, hold the first in the left hand, and knot the other three times over it with the right hand; then take the next four threads, hold three of them in the left hand, and knot the fourth thread three times over them with the right hand. Repeat to the end of desk. Then loosen the third line; hold it in the right hand, and knot each thread twice on to it with the left; then take the first four threads, make a Solomon's knot. Repeat to the end. Take the first two threads and make four single chain, as follows:—Hold the first thread straight in the left hand, knot the other thread on to it with the right hand; then hold this thread straight in the right hand, knot the other on to it with the left; hold this thread in the left hand, knot the other on to it with the right; hold this in the right hand, and knot the other on with the left; take the next two threads, do the same, and repeat with every two threads to

[54]

the end of desk; then miss the first two threads, and with the next four threads make a Solomon's knot. Repeat to the end. Then loosen the fourth line, hold it in the right hand and knot each thread twice on to it with the left. For the first leaf take six threads; hold the first as leader in the right hand over the others, and knot each of the five threads twice on to it with the left hand; then take the first thread again, hold it as before in the right hand, and knot each of the five threads twice on to it with the left. Repeat for two more rows. This forms the first leaf. For the second leaf:—Take six threads; hold the sixth in the left hand over the others, and knot each thread on to it with the right hand. Repeat three more times. Then take the outside thread at each side and make a Solomon's knot with these over all the ten threads; then divide the twelve threads, and hold the sixth thread in the left hand, and knot the other five threads on to it with the right hand. Repeat three times more; and for the fourth leaf:—Take the first thread of the remaining six threads; hold it in the right hand, and knot each of the five threads twice on to it with the left. Repeat three times more; this finishes the star of four leaves. Repeat to the end of cushion; then loosen the fifth line, hold it in the right hand, and knot each thread twice on to it with the left. Then take the first four threads, making a Solomon's knot. Repeat to the end. Then take two threads from each Solomon's knot, and with these make four double chain. This is made same as single, only holding two threads in each hand instead of one. Then loosen the sixth line, hold it in the right hand, and knot each thread twice on to it with the left; then take twelve threads, hold the first in the right hand, and knot each of the eleven threads on to it with the left. Repeat three times more. This forms the first large leaf. Then take the next twelve threads; hold the twelfth in the left hand, and knot each of the eleven threads on to it with the right. Repeat three times more. This forms the second leaf.

Then take the four centre threads, and with them make a raised Picot (this is described in Pattern No. 1); then divide these twenty-four threads into two parts; hold the twelfth thread in the left hand, and knot each thread of the eleventh twice on to it with the right. Repeat three times more; and for the fourth leaf:—Hold the first thread of the twelfth in the right hand, and knot each of the others twice on to it with the left. Repeat three times more. This forms the star of four large leaves. Repeat to the end. Loosen the seventh line, hold it in the right hand, and knot each thread twice on to it with the left.

To Make the Scollop.—Take six threads; hold the first thread in the right hand, and knot the other five threads twice on to it with the left. Pepeat three times more. This forms the first leaf. Then take the next six threads; hold the sixth thread in the left hand, and knot the other five threads on to it with the right hand. Repeat three times more. Join the leaders of both these together, by holding one straight, and knot the other twice over it; then take the next six threads, hold the first thread in the right hand, and knot each of the five threads twice on to it. Repeat three times more to form the leaf. Then take the next six threads, hold the sixth thread in the left hand, and knot the others twice on to it with the right. Repeat three times more. When this leaf is finished hold the leader still in the left hand, and knot six threads twice on to it. Repeat three times more to form the leaf. Then take the six threads that were used in making the second leaf of the scollop; hold the first of these in the right hand, and knot each thread twice on to it with the left. Repeat three times more for the leaf. Then join the leader of this leaf to the leader of the leaf next to it. Repeat till the scollop is completed.

No. 11.

(Threads for this Pattern one yard and twenty-seven inches long.)

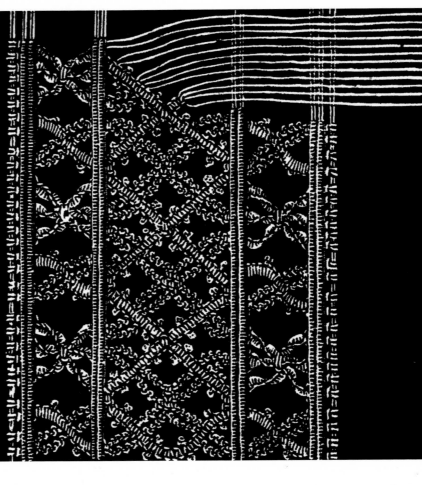

No. 11.

Pin on the lines to the desk in the usual way, after which fasten the threads for working on to the top line. Loosen the second line, hold it in the right hand, and knot each thread twice on to it with the left; then loosen the next line and do the same. Then * take the first four threads, make a Solomon's knot; then with the first two of these threads make four single chain; with the other two threads make three single chain. Then take the next four threads, hold the first three of these in the left hand, and knot the fourth thread four times over them. Then to make the small Picot, make a running knot with the fourth thread, draw it up close to the work, then make another knot in the same way, but let it come inside the first knot, quite close to the work; then with the same thread make four knots over the three threads. Then take these four threads, and the two threads of the single chain close to it, and with the six threads make a Solomon's knot; then take the first four of these, and the two threads of the first single chain, and with the six threads make another Solomon's knot; then take the first four of these threads, hold three of them in the right hand, and knot the first thread four times over them with the left hand; then make a small Picot; after which make four more knots with the same thread over the three threads; then take the next four threads, make eight knots with those, each knot being the first part of the Solomon's knot. This makes a twist. Then take the next four threads, and with them make six knots in the same way. Take the next four threads and make eight knots of the same. Then take these twelve threads, hold the ten centre threads together, and make a

Solomon's knot over them with the two outside threads. Then take the first four of these threads, make eight knots same as before. Take the next four threads, make six knots. Take the next four threads, make eight of the same knots. Repeat from * to the end of desk. Loosen the fourth line, hold it in the right hand, and knot each thread twice on to it with the left. Loosen the next line and do the same. Then take the first four threads, make a Solomon's knot; take the first two of these four threads and make six single chain; take the next two threads, make four chain; miss the next two threads, and with the next four threads make a Solomon's knot. Then take two of these threads and the two threads that were missed, and with them make a Solomon's knot; then make another; then make a small Picot at each side; then make another Solomon's knot with the same threads. Then take these four threads, and the two threads of the single chain close to it, and with the six threads make a Solomon's knot. Then leave out two threads at the right side, and make a Solomon's knot with the four threads. Then take in the two threads of the first single chain, and with the six threads make a Solomon's knot; then leave out two threads, at the right side again, and with the four threads make a Solomon's knot; then make a small Picot at each side; then make three more Solomon's knots; then a small Picot at each side; then another Solomon's knot; then take two of the threads that were left out, and with them make four single chain; then take the other two threads and make four single chain; then take the two threads left at the top of Solomon's knot and the two threads next to it, and make a Solomon's knot; then make another; then a small Picot at each side; then another Solomon's knot; then take four threads, make a Solomon's knot; then take the first two of these threads, make four single chain; then make a Solomon's knot with these two threads and the four threads next to it; then leave out two threads at the left side, and make a Solomon's knot with

the four threads; then with the two top threads make six single chain; then with these two threads, and the four threads close to them, make a Solomon's knot; then take the four threads at the left side, and make four single chain with the first two, and six single chain with the next two; then make a Solomon's knot with the four threads; then take two of these threads, and two from the knot at the left side of them, and with them make a Solomon's knot; then make a Solomon's knot with the four threads of the left side; then make a Solomon's knot with the four threads at the right side; then make a Solomon's knot with the four centre threads; then make a Solomon's knot with the four threads at the left side; then make four single chain with the first two threads, and four single chain with the other two threads; then make a Solomon's knot with the two threads of the first chain and the four threads close to them; then with the first two threads at the left side make six chain, and make a Solomon's knot with the four threads at the right; then take the two threads of the chain at the right side, and the four threads close to them, and with the six threads make a Solomon's knot. Take the two first of these threads and make four single chain; then, with these two threads, and the two close to them at the right side, make a Solomon's knot. This brings the centre pattern close to the fifth line; and when the centre pattern is made to the end of desk, loosen the sixth line, and knot each thread twice on to it. Loosen the next line and do the same; then for the next part repeat from *.

To finish off the Insertion.—Keep the last line pinned on at both ends. Take two threads; draw the second one up under the line in a loop; pass the ends of both threads through this loop, draw them up tight, to form a knot same as the one at the top line. The two threads will now be in front between the two last lines; pass these threads to the back one at each side of the knot; tie them firmly

No. 12

together at the back; sew these threads neatly to the work on the wrong side with a needle and thread. Repeat to the end of desk, and then cut the threads close.

No. 12.

(Threads for this Pattern two yards and eighteen inches long.)

Pin on the lines to the desk, after which fasten the threads for working on the top line. Loosen the next line, hold it in the right hand, and knot each thread twice on to it with the left hand. *Take the first three threads; hold two in the right hand and knot the first thread four times over it with the left hand; then leave a little loop, so:—put a pin between the last knot, and the one now being made; then make four more knots. Take the next three threads; hold two in the left hand and knot the fourth thread eight times over them with the right hand, leaving a loop in the middle same as at the other side. Then to join them, take two threads from each and make one plain knot; then take the three threads at the left side, hold two in the right hand and knot the first thread eight times over them, leaving the little loop in the middle. Then take the other three threads; hold two in the left hand, knot the third thread eight times over them with the right, leaving a loop in the middle. Then take the next four threads; hold the first thread in the right hand, knot the three threads over it with the left. Repeat again to make a leaf. Take the next four threads; hold the fourth thread in the left hand, knot the three threads over it with the right hand. Repeat again. Hold the same leader still in the left hand, and knot the four threads from the left side on to it with the right hand

Repeat again. Then take the other four threads; hold the first of them in the right hand, knot the three threads on to it with the left hand. Repeat again. Repeat from * to the end of desk. Loosen the third line, hold it in the right hand, knot each thread twice on to it with the left hand. Miss the first two threads; take the next two threads, make three single chain; take the next two, make four single chain; take the next two, make six single chain; take the next two, make eight single chain. There will now be twelve threads. Take the first thread; hold it in the right hand, and knot each of the eleven threads twice on to it with the left hand. Repeat for two more rows. Take the first four of these threads; hold the fourth in the left hand, and make a leaf of two rows; pass the leader into the right hand, and make a leaf of two rows. Leave those for the present. Take the next two threads of the twelve; make eight single chain. Take the next thread of the twelve; hold it in the right hand, and knot each of the remaining threads on to it with the left. This part is left for the present. Take up the next six threads; miss the first two; with the next two make three single chain; with the next two make five single chain; then take first of the two that were missed, hold it in the right hand, knot each of the five threads on to it with the left. Repeat for two more rows. Take the next two threads; make five single chain; make three single chain with the next two threads. Take two more threads; hold the second in the left hand, and knot each of the five threads on to it with the left. Repeat for two more rows.

Having described this in detail so far, it is not necessary to continue, as it would only be a repetition of the same thing, and at this stage it would be calculated more to puzzle the worker. The best thing now is to follow the engraving, and when the centre part is made, loosen the

fourth line, hold it in the right hand, and knot each thread twice on to it with the left hand.

To Make the Scollop.—Count off eighteen threads; this will be the centre of the scollop. Count off eighteen threads for the other side of the scollop. Take the two centre threads at the left side, make six single chain; take the next two at the left side, make three chain; take the next two, hold the first in the right hand as leader, and knot each of the five threads on to it twice with the left hand. Repeat for two more rows. Then with six threads from the other side of the scollop do exactly the same, only this time holding the leader in the left hand, and knotting the threads on to it with the right hand; join the two leaders together by holding one, and knotting the other over it twice. Then there will be twelve threads; with every two of these make three single chain. Then take up the next two threads at the left side: hold the second thread in the right hand, and knot the first thread twelve times on to it with the left hand, leaving a loop in the middle by inserting a pin between the threads; then hold the under thread of those two in the right hand as leader, and knot six threads twice on to it with the left. Repeat for two more rows. Then take up the two threads at the other side of the scollop, and do exactly the same, working towards the centre of the scollop. When the third row is made, take four threads at the left side; hold the first in the right hand, knot three threads each twice over it; take four threads at the right side; hold the fourth in the left hand; knot each thread twice on to it with the right hand; join in the middle. Repeat the same at left side. Repeat at right side, until there are five rows, all joined in the middle. Take the first four threads, hold three in the right hand; knot the first thread ten times over them with the left; this will form a thick strand. Do the same at the right side. There are now four threads left at each side from the leaf; take the first two of these, and make seven single chain; make ten with the other two; do the same at the right side. Then commence at the top of the scollop again; left side, take two threads, make six single chain; with the next two make four single chain, and three with the next two. Then take the next two threads; hold the first of these in the right hand; knot seven threads twice on to it with the left hand. Repeat for two more rows. Then take the next two threads, which will be the outside ones; hold the second in the right hand, and knot the first thread ten times on to it with the left hand, leaving a loop in the centre. Take one of these threads; hold it in the right hand as leader, and knot eight threads twice on to it; with the left hand then take up the other thread, which is the last one left; hold it in the right hand, and knot nine threads twice on to it with the left. Then leave out the first four threads.

Take the next thread, hold it in the right hand, knot each thread twice on to it with the left, taking in the first chain. Repeat for two more rows. Miss the first four threads; take the next thread, hold it in the right hand; knot each thread twice on to it with the left, taking in the second single chain. Repeat for two more rows. Miss the first four threads; take up the next thread, hold it in the right hand, knot each thread twice on to it with the left hand, taking in the thick strand. Repeat for two more rows. Miss the first four threads; take up the next thread, hold it in the right hand, knot each thread twice on to it with the left hand. Repeat for two more rows. Leave out four threads again, and with the other four make a strand, so :—Hold three threads in the right hand, and knot the first one eight times over it with the left; then take the first four threads that were left out, hold the first in the right hand, knot the three threads each twice on to it with the left hand. Repeat for two more rows. This forms a small leaf; do exactly the same with each four threads that were left out; there will then be five

leaves. Take the first leaf, hold three of its threads in the right hand; knot the first thread twelve times over them in the left hand, leaving a loop in the centre of them. Then take the four threads of the next leaf and the four threads of the first; hold seven of these threads in the left hand, and knot the first on to them with the left three times; then cut away two threads closely at the back of the work; then knot on the same thread until there are twelve knots, leaving a loop in the centre. Repeat until all the five leaves are worked in. Do exactly the same thing at the right hand side of the scollop, and to finish it at the point, take the six threads left, three from each side, let them cross one over the other, and knot one thread neatly over them, drawing very tight, and cut off the threads at the back, and fasten neatly with a needle and fine thread.

No. 13.

(Threads for this Pattern one yard four inches long.)

Pin on the straight lines in the usual way to the desk; then fasten the threads for working on to the top line. Then loosen the second line at the right side, hold it in the right hand, and knot each thread twice on to it with the left. * Take three threads; hold two in the left hand, and knot the third thread twice over them with the right. Repeat to the end of desk. Leave out the first thread, take up the next three threads; hold the first two in the left hand, knot the third thread twice over them with the right. Repeat to the end of desk. Loosen the third line, hold it in the right hand, knot each thread twice on to it with the left hand. Take the first four threads; hold the fourth thread in the left hand, and knot each of the three threads twice on to it with the

No. 13.

right; pass the same leader to the right hand, knot the threads on with the left, pass the leader back to the left hand, knot the threads on with the right, pass the leader again to the right hand, knot the threads on with the left. This will make four twists. Take the next four threads, make three twists in the same way; take the next four threads, make two twists; take the next four threads, hold the fourth thread in the left hand, and knot all the fifteen threads each twice on to it with the right hand. Repeat for another row; leave this for the present. Take the next four threads; hold the fourth thread in the right hand, knot each of the three threads twice on to it with the right, then pass the leader to the right hand. Repeat to make four twists. Then take four threads at the left side, make a twist of three; take the next four threads, make a twist of three; take the next four threads at the left side, and again make a twist of three; leave this. Commence at the top, miss four threads, take up the next four threads, and with them make a twist of two; take the next four threads, make a twist of three; take the next four threads, make a twist of four, then go back to the four threads that were missed; take the first of these, hold it in the right hand, knot the fifteen threads each twice on to it with the left. Repeat for a second line. Leave out the four threads of these at the right side, and with the next four threads make a twist of three; with the next four threads do the same, and the same with the next four threads; then take up one of the centre threads of the middle twist, hold it in the left hand, and knot nine threads at the left hand side on to it with the right hand; then take up again the centre thread of the middle twist, hold it in the right hand, and knot each of the nine threads on to it with the left; then take six threads from each side; hold eight in the middle, and make a Solomon's knot with the two from each side; this forms half the diamond, and for the lower half repeat the instructions for above; reversing them. Repeat to the end of desk. Then loosen the fourth line, hold it in the

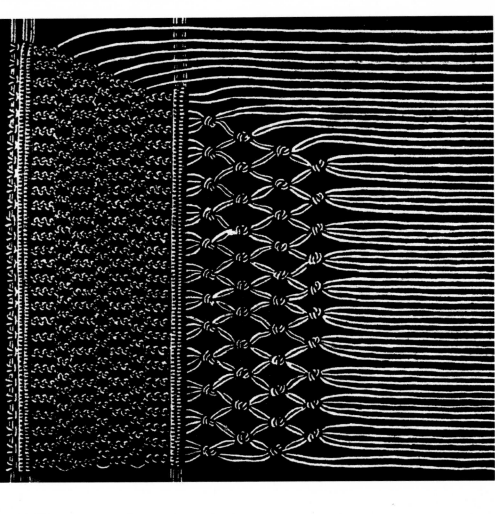

No. 14.

right hand, and knot each thread twice on to it with the left. Repeat from *; after which loosen the fifth line, hold it in the right hand, and knot each thread twice on to it with the left. For the fringe take six threads, and with them make a running knot. Repeat to the end.

No. 14.

(Threads for this Pattern one yard long.)

Pin the straight lines on to the desk in the usual way; then fasten on the threads for working on the top line. Then loosen the second line, hold it in the right hand, and knot each thread twice on to it with the left. Take the first two threads; make four single chain. Repeat for another row. Take the first two threads; make four single chain. Repeat to the end of desk. Miss the first thread and with the two next threads make two single chains. Repeat to the end of desk. Take the first two threads; make four single chain; repeat. Misr the first thread, and with the next two threads make two chain. Repeat to the end of desk. Take the first two threads; make four chain. Miss the first thread and with the next two threads; make two chain; Repeat to end of desk. Take the first two threads; make four chain. Repeat to end of desk. Then loosen the fourth straight line, hold it in the right hand, knot each thread twice over it; loosen the next straight line, hold it in the right hand, knot each thread twice on to it with the left; and for the fringe, take four threads and with them make a running knot; draw it up to within a quarter of an ineh of the last straight line. Repeat to end of desk. Miss the two first threads; make a similar knot with the next four threads. Repeat to end of desk. Make two more rows of knots.

This makes a handsome fringe, and is especially adapted for medium sized thread.

No. 15.

(Threads for this Pattern one yard and twenty-seven inches long.)

Pin the straight lines on to the desk in the usual way, and fasten the threads for working on to the top line. Loosen the second line, hold it in the right hand, knot each thread twice on it. Take the first four threads; make two double chain. Repeat to the end. Then loosen the third line, hold it in the right hand, knot each thread twice on to it with the left hand. Take three threads; hold the first thread in the right hand, knot two on to it with the left hand; take the next three threads, hold the third in the left hand, knot three on to it with the right hand; take the first thread, hold it in the right hand; knot three threads on to it with the left. Repeat at each side, until there are five rows to each leaf; then take the six threads, make a Solomon's knot, repeat to the end of desk. Loosen the fourth line, hold it in the right hand, knot each thread twice on to it with the left. Take the first two threads, with them make five single chain. Take the next four threads; hold the fourth thread in the left hand, knot the three threads twice over it. Take the next four, hold the fourth in the left hand, knot each of the nine threads over it with the right: repeat for two more rows. Take the first two of these threads. Make four chain; make three chain with all the other threads: leave those for the present. Take four threads; make a Solomon's knot; take two of these threads, make four single chain; do the same with the other two threads. Take the first of these four threads; hold it in the left hand, knot eight threads

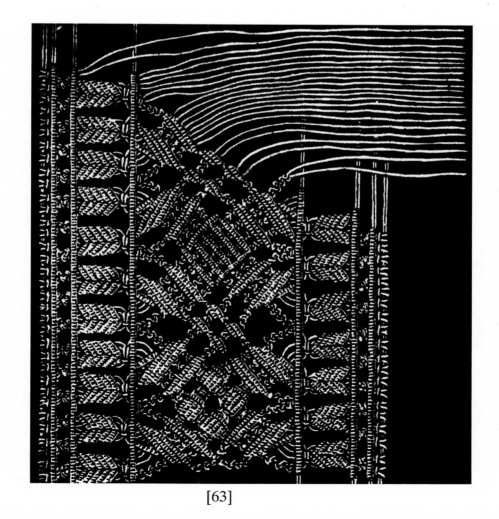

No. 15.

hand, knot eight threads on to it with the left ; take the next thread, do the same ; take these eight threads, and with every two of them make three chain. Take up one thread of the single chain at the beginning, hold it in the right hand, knot eight threads over it. Repeat for two more rows. Take the two first threads of these, make six single chain ; take the next four threads, hold the first in the right hand, knot three threads over it ; loosen the fifth straight line, hold it in the right hand, knot each thread twice on to it with the left.

The remainder of the centre patterns can be made by following the engraving, as it is almost all a repetition of what has been described, and the pattern at the top is repeated at the bottom of the Insertion, only reversing the order of working ; and for fastening off the threads, see Instructions No. IV., Insertion Pattern.

No. 16.

(Threads for this Pattern two yards long.)

Pin on the threads in the usual way to the desk, and to make the Picot heading. Take two threads, hold the ends of them evenly together, then pin them on to the desk above the first line, and make with them two double chain over the pin. Repeat to the end of desk. Then loosen the first line at the right side, hold it in the right hand, and knot each thread twice on to it with the left ; then make three rows of Solomon's knots to the end of the desk. Then loosen the second line, hold it in the right hand, knot each thread twice on to it with the left ; take the first two threads, make eight chain ; * take the next twelve threads, make three Solomon's knots, and under these make three more accord-

over it with the right hand, take the next of the four threads, hold it in the left hand, knot ten threads over it with the right hand ; take the first two of these threads, and make six single chain ; make three chain with the next two threads ; take the next four threads, make a Solomon's knot, the same with the next four threads ; leave for the present. Take up twelve threads, and with the last four of them make a Solomon's knot ; make four single chain with each two of these threads ; take the next four of them, hold the first in the right hand, knot each of the three threads on to it : with the left take the next four of them, hold the first thread in the right hand, knot nine threads on to it with the left ; repeat for two more rows ; take the first two of these threads, make three single chain. Do the same with the other six threads. Take one of the threads from the single chain at the left side, hold it in the right hand, knot eight threads on to it with the left ; take up the other thread of the single chain, hold it in the right hand, knot eight threads on to it with the left, make two Solomon's knots with those eight threads. Take the fourth thread of the second Solomon's knot at the left side of this, hold it in the right hand, and knot four threads on to it with the left. Repeat for three more rows ; take the top thread of these four rows, hold it in the left hand, knot the three threads over it ; with the right hand then make a Solomon's knot with these four threads, and do the same with the other four threads ; this forms a small medallion. Take four of these threads at the right side, and the four threads next to it ; make another medallion ; then take two Solomon's knots with the eight threads ; then take the remaining four threads of the first medallion with the four threads next to it ; make another medallion ; then make two Solomon's knots with the eight threads ; then take four threads of these, and four of the second medallion, and make another medallion ; then make two Solomon's knots with the eight threads ; take up the thread at the side of the third medallion, hold it in the right

No. 16.

ing to the engraving. Take the first of these twelve threads, hold it in the right hand, knot five threads on to it with the left; take the last of these twelve threads, hold it in the left hand, knot six threads on to it with the right; make five single chain with every two of these threads. Leave these for the present. Take up four threads; hold the first in the right hand, knot the three threads on to it with the left. Repeat for three more rows, to form a leaf. Take the next four threads, hold the fourth in the left hand, dnot the three threads on with the right hand. Repeat from * to the end of desk.

Tape up the second thread; hold it in the right hand, knot six threads on to it with the left hand; take up the first thread, knot six threads on in the same way. Take up the first thread of the first leaf, hold it in the left hand, knot six threads on to it with the right; take the next thread of the leaf; do the same. Then take the first leader at the left side, hold it in the right hand, and knot the first leader at the right side twice on to it; lo the same with the other two leaders. Then under the two leaves make a Solomon's knot with four threads, take the fourth thread of the second leaf, hold it in the right hand, knot six threads on to it with the left, take the remaining thread of the leaf, hold in the right hand; do the same. Then with those sixteen threads make fifteen more Solomon's knots, making in all sixteen; take up the second leader at the left side, hold it in the right hand, knot eight threads on to it with the left; take up the first leader, and do the same; take the seventh thread, hold it in the left hand, knot the six threads on to it with the right; take up the eighth thread, hold it in the left hand, knot the seven threads on to it with the right hand; take the first two of these threads, make ten single ceain; take the next two threads, make five single chain; do the same with the ten remaining threads; take the seventh thread, hold it in the left hand, knot the six threads over it with the right; take up the eighth thread, hold it in the right hand, knot five

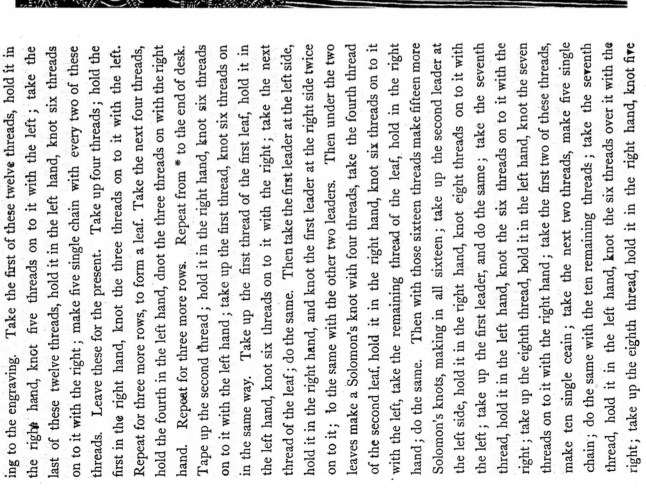

[65]

remaining eight threads ; this forms a diamond. Repeat from * until there are ten diamonds, according to the engraving, to form the scollop.

No. 17.

The lace is made by knotting the threads together, the rule to be observed being to take one thread as a leader, hold it firmly, and knot each single thread twice on to it, always keeping the leader at the top. When the leaf is worked from right to left, the leader is held in the left hand, and when the leaf is worked from left to right, the leader is held in the right hand.

Cut the cross lines the length of the lace required, fasten them on the desk with the largest pins ; the threads for this pattern are to be one yard four inches long.

INSTRUCTIONS.

Fasten the threads on as follows: Pass the two ends of each thread under the first line, pointing them up, then draw them back through the loop. Then put in a pin between every four threads. Loosen the second line at the right side, hold it in the right hand, and knot each thread twice on to it with the left hand.

First line of open work: Take the first four threads, hold three in the left hand, and knot the fourth thread three times over them with the right hand; so on to the end. Then take two threads from each, hold three in the right hand and knot the fourth three times over them with the left hand. Then loosen the third line, hold it in the right hand and knot each thread twice on to it.

threads on to it with the left. Then with those twelve threads make nine Solomon's knots according to the engraving. Take up the first of these threads ; hold it in the right hand ; knot five threads on to it with the left, do the same on the other side, holding the leader in the left hand and knotting the threads on with the right. Repeat from * to the end of desk. Then loosen the third straight line, hold it in the right hand, knot each thread on to it with the left. Then take four threads, make two Solomon's knots. Repeat to end. Miss two threads, take the next four threads ; make two Solomon's knots. Repeat to end. Loosen the fourth line, hold it in the right hand ; knot each thread on to it with the left.

To Make the Scollop.—*Take the first two threads, make six single chain ; take the next two threads, make four single chain ; make two single chain with the next ; take up two threads, hold the second in the left hand, knot seven threads over it with the right. Repeat for another row. Take up eight threads, make five chain with the last two of them ; make four chain with the next, and two chain with the next ; take up the first of these eight threads ; hold it in the right hand, knot seven threads on to it with the left. Repeat for another row. Then with twelve of these threads make nine Solomon's knots according to the engraving. Then take up the first thread ; hold it in the right hand ; knot seven threads on to it with the left. Repeat for another row. Take the last thread ; hold it in the left hand ; knot seven threads on to it with the right. Repeat for another row. Then take the leader from the other side, and knot twice on to this leader ; then take the first of these threads, make three single chain, do the same with the next six threads ; then miss the first thread ; take the two next threads, and make three chain ; do the same to the next two threads, and the same to the following two threads ; then make six single chain with every two of the

No. 18

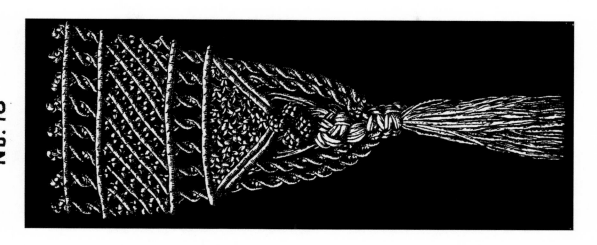

No. 17

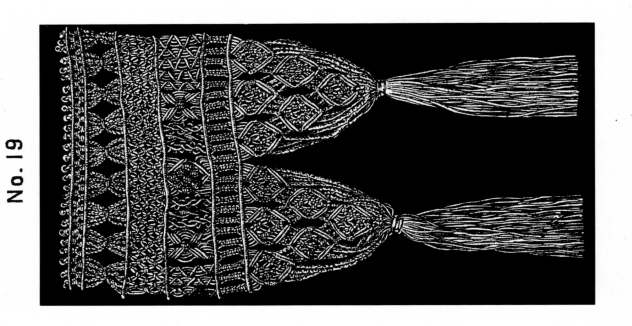

No. 23

No. 19

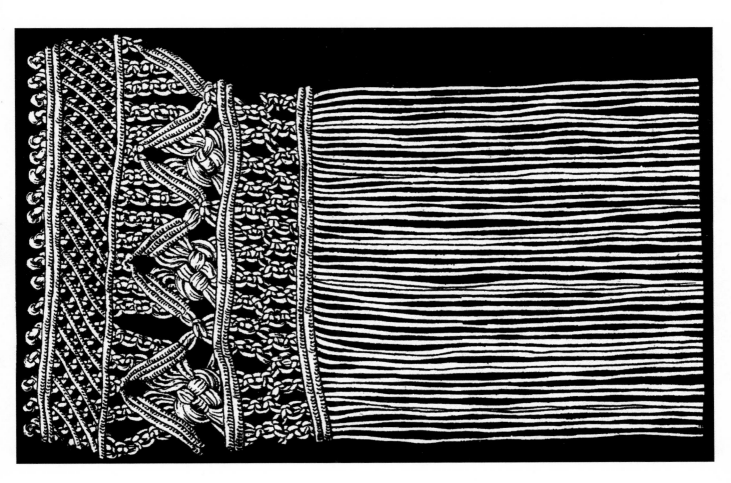

To make the first leaf: Take eight threads, hold the eighth one in the left hand as leader, knot each of the seven threads twice on to it with the right hand, always keeping the leader at the top and the threads underneath. Then take the eighth again, hold it in the left hand and knot the seven threads twice on to it with the right; the third line of the leaf is made in the same way; repeat for the second and third leaf. Fourth leaf: hold the thread at the left side in the right hand as leader, and knot the threads on to it with the left hand. Then take the fourth line and knot each thread twice on to it in the same way; second line of open work same as the first, then take the fifth line and knot each thread twice on to it.

First leaf of scollop; take eight threads, hold the eighth one in the left hand as leader, and make the leaf same as the first one in the insertion.

When this leaf is finished, pass the leader to the right hand and make the second leaf. Third leaf: hold the leader in the right hand and knot on the threads with the left. Fourth leaf: pass the leader of the third leaf to the left hand, and knot on the threads with the right hand. When this leaf is finished, knot the leader twice on to the leader of the second leaf. The remainder of the scollop is made in the same way, as may be seen by the engraving.

No. 23

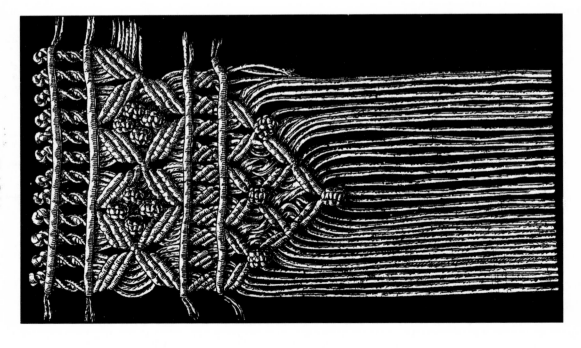

MACRAME BAG, EARLY 20TH C.
from collection of LACIS MUSEUM OF LACE AND TEXTILES [COG.14713]

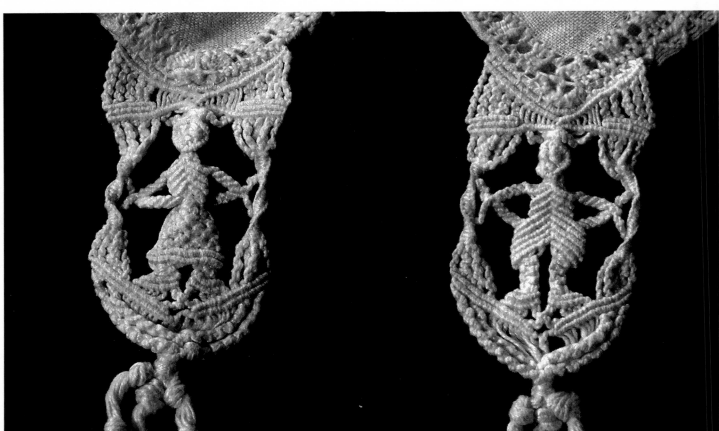

Macrame Pillow Cover Insesrt and Tassels, 19th c.
from collection of Lacis Museum of Lace and Textiles [JIG.14811]

The
Priscilla Macramé Book

A COLLECTION OF HANDSOME DESIGNS

WITH

Directions for Working

EDITED BY

BELLE ROBINSON

PRICE, 25 CENTS

PUBLISHED BY

The Priscilla Publishing Company

85 BROAD STREET, BOSTON, MASS.

No. 750. MACRAMÉ COLLAR. See description, page 12

MACRAMÉ AND HOW TO MAKE IT

MACRAMÉ does not need any introduction as new work, but it does need introduction to new people. It is about twenty-five years since the last revival of this most fascinating handiwork. If search is made for the origin of Macramé, its claims of great antiquity can be substantiated. The name, as we have it, is of Arabic origin, and the work in the heavier grades has been used, lavishly, to decorate and finish the edges of trappings, tents, etc. The Italians first adapted its use to finer threads, the making of laces and fine fringes.

EQUIPMENT.—The requisite tools for Macramé are to be found in any sewing-basket. A crochet-needle, for occasional use in drawing groups of threads through knots; needle and thread for fastening threads at the back of the work; a pair of sharp scissors; a few dozen of pins, preferably those with black or white heads; and a heavy cushion upon which to mount the work. A floor cushion, burlap-covered (see Fig. 1), and with a piece of cheesecloth pinned over it, is suggested. A light, soft pine frame, or stretcher (about 20 x 24), can be used to advantage if a yard of burlap is pinned about it. Then 24 inches can be pinned down or mounted at once. In the case of the waste-paper basket (page 15), such a stretcher was filled twice for the 48 inches of fringe around the top. A thin board, 6 x 24 inches, covered with cloth padded with excelsior, and with loops at the upper corners to hang to a chair-back, is a convenient mount. Sometimes small nails are driven at equal distances in a board of soft wood. If they are properly spaced they answer as a substitute for pins, but there is no easy way to pin down the work as it progresses, and that is important and sometimes necessary.

When threads are so long as to be troublesome, they may be wound over two fingers into a tiny skein and secured by very small safety-pins, or the thread may be wound on a bit of cardboard, notched at each end.

THREADS.—Many varieties of thread are adapted to the work. The Macramé cords come in Nos. 6, 9, and 12, No. 6 being the finest. Silk cord is used, and firmly twisted crochet cottons are admirable in Nos. 2, 3, 5, and 10. Loosely twisted crochet cotton No. 5 makes good work (see Card Case, page 26). Pearl cotton No. 3 was used for Belt No. 773 and Figs. 40 and 41.

STITCHES or KNOTS. — The number of actual stitches or knots are few, but the combinations of them are endless. Definitions of some of the terms will be given before describing the stitches.

Abbreviations.—Ch—chain; st—stitch; p—picot; k—knot; coll k—collecting knot; thd—thread; hor—horizontal; bull—bullion; dbl—double; diag—diagonal; bh—buttonhole.

Cord.— The thd held taut in either hand while, with the other hand, thds are knotted around it.

Knotting Threads.—The thds coiled around the cords, or knotted with each other. Cords and knotting thds may be exchanged, since the distinction is only temporary.

Bar.—The result of knotting or coiling any number of threads each twice around a cord. Bars may be hor, diag to the left or right, or vertical.

Double and Triple Bars.—Two or three bars in the same direction and very close together. A bar is called a "cordon," a "Barrette," a "Baguette," etc.

Cordon Stitch.—Two coils of a single knotting thd around a cord. Bars are composed of Cordon sts but that name is used only when a single thd is coiled. This st has been wrongly described as a bh st, but it is better to have a distinctive name, since there is a difference. A bh st may be made with one thd lying beside another, whereas in making the Cordon st, the cord is held above the knotting thd and the knotting thd always crosses under the cord before making the two coils.

A Simple Hard Knot or Tight Knot.—The thd looped over itself and the end brought up through the loop.

A Binding Knot.—Two or more thds held together and tied (as above) in a hard k. Other terms are explained in connection with the illustrations of sts.

Figure 2. Mounting of Working Threads over a single cord, sometimes it is advisable to use a double cord. The thd is doubled, the loop put over the cord, the ends brought down through the loop and finally drawn tight.

Figure 3. Mounting Completed and secured by a Hor Bar. The two coils of the 6th thd give a good representation of the Cordon st.

Figure 4. Mounting and Bar completed.

Figure 5. Second Mounting.—In this the loop of doubled thd is carried up under the cord and down outside, the ends are brought through the loop towards the worker and drawn tightly. Then a coil is made to the left and one to the right, and when all are tightly drawn it makes a smooth bar, without the purl of the first mount. It is really the first mount "wrong side out" or reversed.

Figure 6 is mounted with a *picot* on every alternate thd. A pin is placed above the cord, a hard k tied over the pin with the middle of the thd. Each end makes a Cordon st, and the 2d thd

FIG. 1. METHOD OF MOUNTING

3

FIG. 2. FIRST MOUNT. See page 3

FIG. 3. HORIZONTAL BAR. See page 3

FIG. 4. MOUNT AND BAR COMPLETE
See Figs. 2 and 3

FIG. 5. SECOND MOUNT. See page 3

is mounted with the second mount (Fig. 5).

Figure 7 employs 4 thds (8 ends). After mounting, the 1st thd (at the left) is taken as cord and held by the right hand in a perfect diag above the other 7 thds, which are taken in turn by the left hand to make the bar. After all the thds are used, the cord is taken in the left hand and held diagonally to the left while the process is repeated, with the right hand manipulating the knotting thds.

Too much emphasis cannot be placed upon the fact that one must learn to use both hands in Macramé. At first that may seem hard to do, but a little effort and repeated practice will give to the left hand skill almost, perhaps quite, equal to that of the right hand.

Figure 8. Triple and Double Bars.—The 6th thd (at the right) is used for cord. When the first bar is finished, the 6th thd (the last that falls at the right) is used for cord, and that which was the first cord is knotted on at the last end of the bar. This is to be repeated to make the third bar. Sometimes where cords cross the thds at right angles, each cord is taken up in turn and let fall at the last end of the bar, without becoming a knotting thd. The third cord (in this case) is turned and makes the first cord of the dbl

diag bar to the right. The first thd at the left becomes the second cord, and at the lower right hand of the cut is shown the first cord of the bar knotting and finishing the second bar. If the beginner is ever at a loss to know which hand holds the cord in any given figure (and that may easily occur), it may be decided by remembering this,—Whichever way the bar is to run, right or left (whether horizontally or diagonally) that hand is to hold the cord. Having this fixed one need never hesitate.

Figure 9. Linen Stitch.—Two threads (4 ends) are mounted. After the first Hor Bar, a heading is made of 1 Flat-st (see Fig. 10) and a second bar follows this. Of the 2 thds at the left, the Coll K is made with the right thd; at the right, the k is made with the left thd. Solid cloth like the diamonds in No. 784, may be made with this st.

Figure 10. Flat Stitch.—The heading is Linen st in three rows followed by a bar. At the left the Flat-st is made over 2 thds, at the right over 1. Below is shown the two throws that compose this st. Where 1 Flat-st is directed always means both throws.

Figure 11.—The heading is one Cordon st to the right with first 2 thds, and one to the

FIG. 6. PICOT MOUNT, OR VENETIAN PICOT. See page 3

4

left with 3d and 4th thds, a Coll K with 2d and 3d, Cordon st to the left with 1st and 2d, Cordon st to the right with 3d and 4th, Hor Bar, after which a Single Ch of 2 thds is made as follows: One bh st with right thd over left thd, then the right thd is held taut and a bh st is made over it with the left thd. One Ch st includes both throws. At B 2 thds are held in one hand and the work of Fig. 11 A is repeated.

Figure 12.—The heading at A is a diagonal bar to the left, made over the 4th thd as cord. Below the second bar are Bull sts to right and left. To make 1 Bull st: * bring the 2d thd under the 1st and make the st *. Repeat from * to *. The cord and knotting thd are in this way exchanged after each st. The 2d thd held above for cord and the 1st drawn under for knotting thd turns the Bull to the left.

At **B**, 2 thds are held in each hand and the Dbl Bull turns to the right, it can be made to the left also.

Figure 13, A. Spiral Stitch.—Repeating the first half of Flat-st with 4 thds makes Spiral st or Bannister bars.

Figure 13, B.—Basket Stitch is made with 4 thds. * With the 4th make a bh st over the 2d and 3d, then with the 1st make a bh st over the 2d and 3d. Repeat from *.

Figure 14, A.— Double Buttonhole is made by 1 bh st with the left thd over the right thd and one with the left thd under the right thd. The two throws make 1 dbl bh st. Or they may be made by the right thd over and under the left. Both are given at Fig. 14, A.

Figure 14, B.—Waved Buttonhole is made with 4 thds, always working over the 2 middle thds. Five bh sts with the left thd over the 2 middle, and 5 bh sts with the right thd over the 2 middle.

Figure 15. Mounting with Chain Picot.—Two thds, with middle of loops pinned together above the cord, and 2 Ch sts made with each pair of thds, then the thds mounted on a Hor Bar, make this mounting. One thread is doubled and mounted (2d mount) after each p.

Figure 16. Large Picot Mounting.— Each thd is tied in a hard k in the middle. This k is pinned down and a Coll K made with the right thd. For

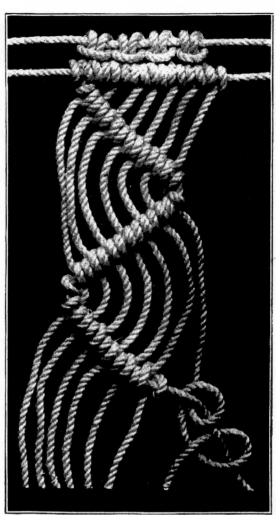

FIG. 7. RIGHT AND LEFT DIAGONAL BARS
See page 4

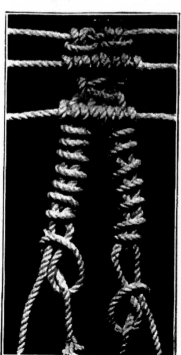

FIG. 9. COLLECTING KNOT OR LINEN STITCH. See page 4

FIG. 8. TRIPLE BARS TO LEFT AND DOUBLE BARS TO RIGHT
See page 4

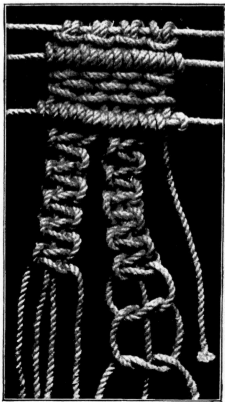

FIG. 10. FLAT-STITCH OVER TWO THREADS AND OVER ONE THREAD
See page 4

5

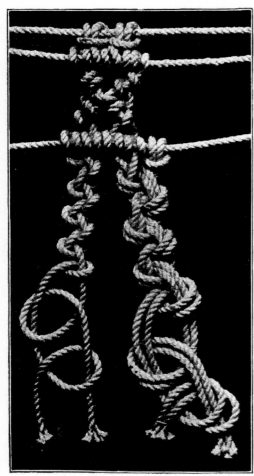
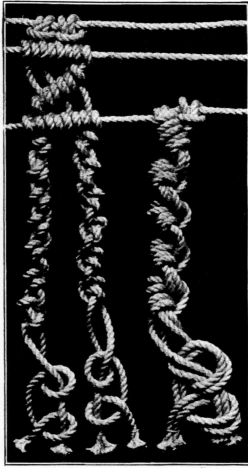

FIG. 11, A.—CHAIN STITCH. B.—DOUBLE
CHAIN STITCH. See page 4

FIG. 12, A—BULLION STITCH. B—DOUBLE
BULLION STITCH. See page 5

Fig. 17. * Make 5 bh sts, a p (hard knot) pinned down *. Make from * to * twice more, then 5 bh sts. Leaving these ends mount two more p on the bar, then mount the last ends of the scallop. Mount 1 p on the bar between scallops.

Figure 19. Binding off an Edge.—When a band of Macramé is made for insertion, with the thds mounted along one edge, the other edge is usually finished with a bar and the thds turned back and sewed. A finish that is shown at Fig. 19 (page 7) and more nearly resembles the first edge, may be made as follows: Turn the piece wrong side up, so that the lower left corner, A, becomes the upper right corner. With the left hand turn the 1st thd back on the work, with the 2d thd make a bh st over the 1st thd and lay the 2d along the 1st. With the 3d make a bh st over the 1st and 2d. Lay the 3d along the 2d (dropping the

the large p, two of these k are pinned a little space apart and a Flat-st made with 4 thds and the ends mounted on a Hor Bar. The next thd is mounted just after the Coll K is made, and is a small p.

Figure 17. Buttonhole Scallops.—To mount, make 10 bh sts with the middle of one thd over another, mount the first two ends on Hor Bar. Mount a thd like 2d mount, then mount the last ends of the first 2 thds. Mount another thd (2d mount) and repeat from the first.

Figure 18. Scallops and Picots.— Mount 1 p like smaller p in Fig. 16. Mount 2 thds as in scallops of

FIG. 13, A.—SPIRAL STITCH. B.—BASKET
STITCH. See page 5

FIG. 14, A—DOUBLE BUTTONHOLE STITCH.
B—WAVED BUTTONHOLE STITCH. See page 5

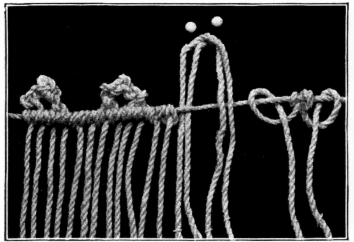

FIG. 15. CHAIN PICOT MOUNTING. See page 5

FIG. 16. LARGE PICOT MOUNTING. See page 5

FIG. 17. MOUNTING WITH BUTTONHOLE SCALLOPS
See page 6

FIG. 18. MOUNTING WITH SCALLOPS AND VENETIAN
PICOT. See page 6

last ends of the first 2 thds are mounted. One thd is mounted with Venetian p, Fig. 6, then another scallop.

Figure 20, B.—To mount with scallops of single thread, as in Fig. 20 B, two loops are pinned close to the cord, the first end of the 1st thd mounted on the bar, the first end of the 2d thd is mounted next. The second end of the 2d thd follows, then the second end of the 1st thd.

Figure 21, A—Triangle Stitch, and Fig. 21, B—Square Stitch.—The method of making these two sts is given clearly in the illustration.

Figure 22, A. Shell of Flat Stitch.—The shell is made with 4 thds. After 4 Flat-sts are finished the two knotting thds are crossed and each end drawn down (with a crochet-hook) just above the 1st Flat-st. At Fig. 22, B, the shell is made with 8 thds in the same way. At Fig. 22, C, after 3 Dbl Ch sts are finished, the thds are drawn to the back of the work.

Figure 24, A.—This shows the gimp of Single Bar, which is the foundation of Fig. 23. A Cordon st is made to the right, the thd pinned down in a p and the thd passed under the cord to the left, a Cordon st to the left, thd pinned in p, thd to the right and Cordon st to the right, etc. With two bars spaced any distance apart, the gimp is made wider.

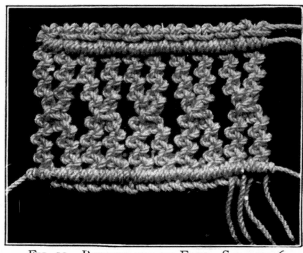

FIG. 19. BINDING OFF AN EDGE. See page 6

1st) and with the 4th make a bh st over the 2d and 3d. Lay the 4th along the 3d (dropping the 2d), and with the 5th make a bh st over the 3d and 4th. The thds are to be sewed tightly, or, if the work is solid, they may be left cut one-half inch long and they will stay turned back from the edge.

Figure 20, A.—To mount the double buttonhole scallop and Venetian Picot of Fig. 20, A, 7 dbl Bh sts are made with the middle of one thd over another. The first ends are mounted on a bar, one thd is mounted (2d mount), then the

7

FIG. 20, A. MOUNTING OF DOUBLE BUTTONHOLE AND VENETIAN PICOT. See page 7

FIG. 20, B. MOUNTING WITH SCALLOPS OF SINGLE THREAD. See page 7

Figure 24, B. Four-Strand Sennit is the cord made for Hand Bag No. 756. Two thds, doubled and giving 4 ends, are pinned down. * The outer right thd is carried under two thds and back over one, the outer left thd under two and back over one *. Repeat from * to *. In the illustration the next step is,—outer left thd under two and back (to the left) over one.

On pages 10 and 11 are given twenty-four bands of knotting that may be used in various ways, as cords, etc. From three to six thds are employed in the different bands. Many variations of these may be made, these are suggestive.

Figure 25, A.—Three thds — Double Bar to the left, Coll K with right over middle thd, Dbl Bar to the right, Coll K with left over middle thd.

Figure 25, B—Three thds—One Ch st with the right and middle thds, one Ch st with middle and left thds.

Figure 25, C — Four thds — Six times, the first half of Flat-st and six times, the second half of Flat-st.

Figure 25, D — Three thds — Linen st or Coll K. One k with 2d and 3d, one k with 1st and 2d.

Figure 25, E—Three thds — Diag Bars to the left.

Figure 25, F — Three thds — Zig-zag st. Hor Bar to the left, with the same cord Hor Bar to the right. May be made with 2 or any number of thds.

Figure 25, G—Three thds—Double bh st with right thd over 1st and 2d, Dbl bh st with left thd over 2d and 3d.

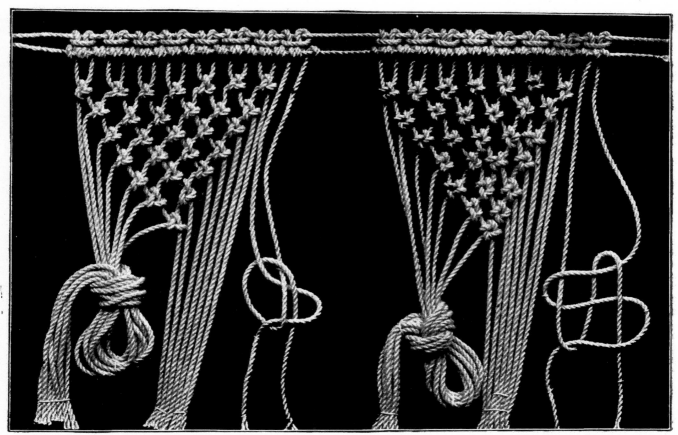

FIG. 21, A. TRIANGLE STITCH. See page 7

FIG. 21, B. SQUARE STITCH. See page 7

8

Figure 26, A — Four thds — Flat-st, Dbl bh with 2d thd over 1st, Dbl bh with 3d thd over 4th.

Figure 26, B — Four thds — Double bh with 2d over 1st and with 3d over 4th. After each st the knotting thds cross, as seen below.

Figure 26, C — Three thds — Double bh with 3d over middle and the same with 1st over middle.

Figure 26, D — Three thds — Six bh sts with 3d over 1st and 2d, Venetian P. Repeat with the same thd and the twist forms itself.

Figure 26, E — Three thds — Shell Buttonhole. Five bh sts with 3d over 1st and 2d, bring 3d over to the left and make 5 bh sts with thd brought up from the right.

Figure 26, F—Three thds—Picot Bar. With 3d thd make a Dbl bh st over 1st and 2d, pass 3d under to the left, 2 Dbl bh sts with Venetian P between, pass thd under to right and make 2 Dbl bh sts with P between.

Figure 26, G — Four thds—Four-strand Sennit (see page 9).

Figure 27.—Four thds are used in each band of Fig. 27.
A — One Flat-st, 2 Dbl bh sts with 2d thd over 1st, 2 with 3d over 4th, Coll K with 2d and 3d, 2 Dbl bh sts each way as before.

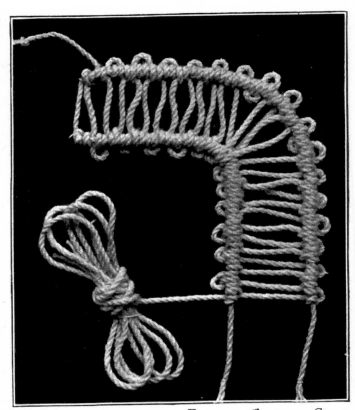

FIG. 23. GIMP OF CUSHION COVER NO. 751

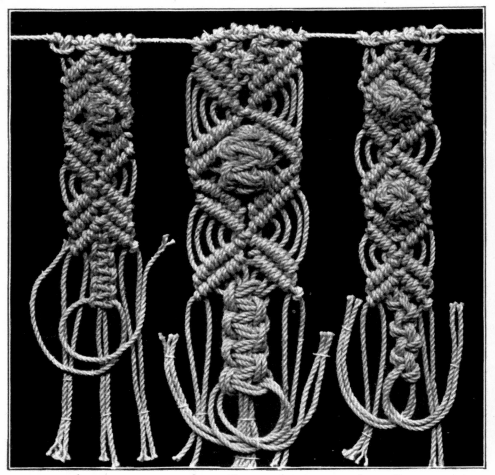

A   B   C
FIG. 22, A. SHELL OF FLAT-STITCH, FOUR THREADS. FIG. 22, B. SHELL OF FLAT-STITCH, EIGHT THREADS. FIG. 22, C. SHELL OF DOUBLE CHAIN STITCH, FOUR THREADS. See page 7

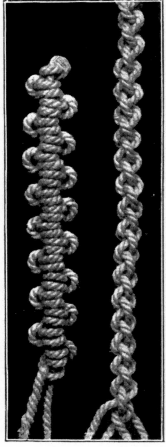

A   B
FIG. 24, A. SINGLE GIMP FIG. 24, B. FOUR-STRAND SENNIT. See pages 7, 8

9

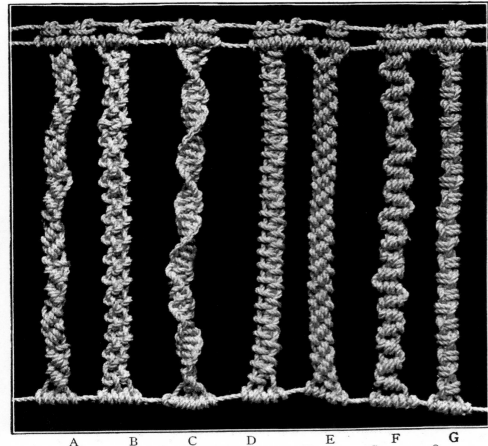

A   B   C   D   E   F   G

FIG. 25. BANDS OF THREE OR FOUR THREADS. See page 8

edge, 3 Flat-sts. Repeat from *.

C—One Flat-st, Diag Bars to left and right, Coll K with 2 middle thds, * 2 Coll K below, Dbl bh with 2d over 1st and 5th over 6th, Coll K between *. From * to * twice more, 2 Coll K, then 1 Coll K below. Finish the medallion with bars to right and left, using outer thds as cords.

D—One Coll K with 2 middle thds, Dbl Bars to left and right with middle thds as cords, Coll K with 2 middle thds, Dbl bh st with 2d over 1st, and with 5th over 6th, Dbl Diag Bars to right and left.

E—Coll K with 2 middle thds, Dbl Bars to right and left, using outer thds for cords, Coll K and 3 Ch sts with 2 middle thds, 6 Dbl bh sts with 1st over 2d and with 6th over 5th, the bars are reversed and at the outer edge a Venetian P is made.

Figure 29. Mounting for Open Design.—Mount, leaving the space

B—One Flat-st, 3 Ch sts with each pair of thds.

C—One Flat-st, with each pair of thds 8 bh sts, Venetian P after the 4th.

D—Two Dbl bh sts with 2d over 1st and the same with 3d over 4th, **2d and 3d tied in a Coll K.**

E—One Flat-st, 3 Dbl bh sts with 2d over 1st and the same with 3d over 4th.

Figure 28—Six thds are used in each band of Fig. 28.

A—Eight Spiral sts are made with the two outer thds over 4, then Linen st for 7 rows.

B—One Flat-st with 2 outer thds over 4, with each group of 3 make * Fig. 26, **C**, until there are 4 sts at the outer edge and 3 at the inner

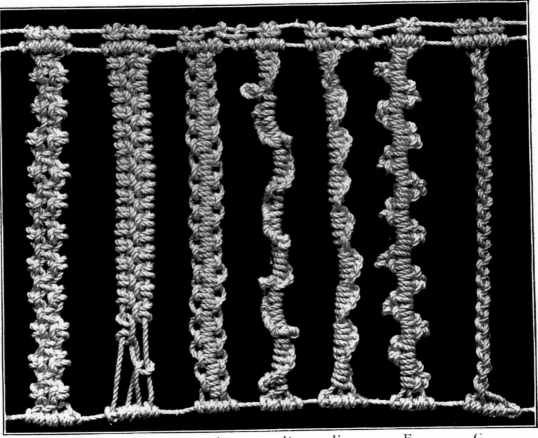

A   B   C   D   E   F   G

FIG. 26. BANDS OF THREE OR FOUR THREADS. See page 9

of one doubled thd between thds, and when making the Hor Bar make three coils instead of two.

Figure 31. Japanese Knots. — Of the 8 knots, B, C, and E are shown clearly in the cut, and diagrams of the other five are given. To make the braid (K) of a single strand, turn the end up and pass under the strand from left to right and pin down. * Bring the end down through the loop and out at the left, twist the loop from right to left, bringing the end over, down through and out at the right. Twist the loop from left to right *. Repeat.

No. 751. Pillow Cover. — This cover requires two balls No. 12 Macramé Cord and one ball of No. 6. The measure of the pillow is 21 x 21. A gimp ½-inch wide is made of No. 12 cord (see Fig. 23). This forms a square frame, 18 in. each side, within which the net is made of Fl-st and Dbl Bars alternating. Three rows of crochet of No. 6 cord finish the outer edge of the cover

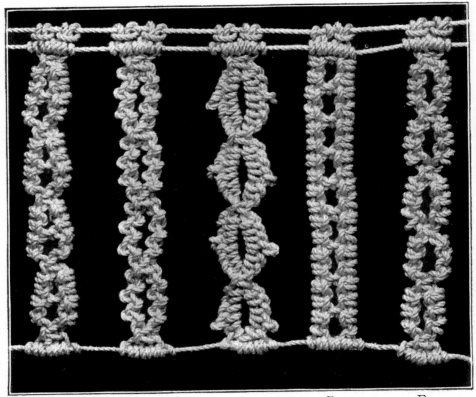

A   B   C   D   E

FIG. 27. BANDS OF FOUR THREADS. See page 9

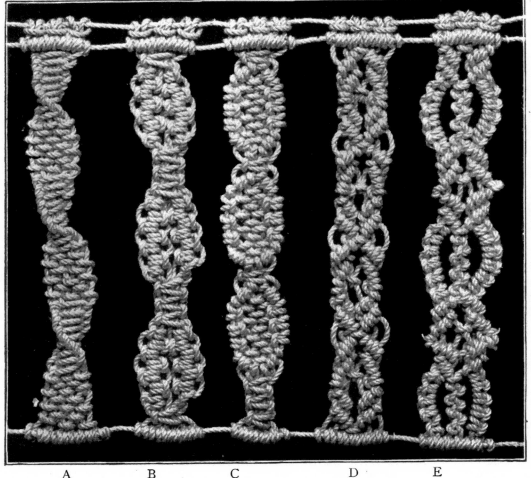

A   B   C   D   E

FIG. 28. BANDS OF SIX THREADS. See page 10

For the gimp cut a cord about 5 yds long and dbl. Use the ball for knotting thd (see Fig. 23, page 9). Inside the square 61 p are required for each side. Pin the square frame as suggested on page 3 and make the net as follows: Cut 40 thds each 3 yds long. With a coarse crochet-hook draw one thd (to the middle) through the first p at the left upper corner and also through the first p down the left side. Repeat this at the last p of the upper side and first p down the right side. Omitting 2 p, mount 2 doubled thds every 3d p all across. *1st row* — Make a Fl-st with each group of four. Draw the first 2 thds at the left through the 3d p down the side, the 1st thd down and the 2d thd up. Repeat at the right side. *2d row* — Letting the first 2 thds hang, make Dbl Diag Bars with each group of 4 thds. Alternate these two

FIG. 29. MOUNT FOR OPEN DESIGN. See page 10

DETAIL OF FIG. 31 A

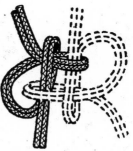

DETAIL OF FIG. 31 D

rows. **Crocheted Edge.** *1st row—* —Eight ch, 1 long treble (1 tr) (3 loops) in the second p, * 3 ch, 1 l tr in 2d p *. *2d row—* * Three double (d) over each ch, 1 ch *. *3d row—* * Single (s) over Ch st below (taking up back loop only), p of 3 ch, 2 ch *.

Frontispiece. No. 750. Collar.— *Materials.—*Four balls medium Macramé cord. Measurements: Depth in back, 9¼ in. Neck-line, 24 in. Between ends of neck-line, 11 in.

Cut 29 2-yd thds, 72 1½-yds, 26, 1-yd thds, mounting the longest thds in the middle and half the others each side. Cut 3 cords 3 yds long, dbl, and begin the work at the middle of the cords and work both ways. Mount with ch p, of 5 ch, mounting 1 thd (2d mount) between p and within each p. *1st row—*Fl-st, commencing with middle four thds. *2d row—*Bar. *3d row—*One Cordon st with 2 middle thds, first as cord and second as knotting thd; * let hang 2 thds, Cordon st with next 2 *, repeat. *4th row—*Bar. *5th row—*One small medallion (Med) of 6 thds in the middle, 8 Med each side, 4 half Med beyond at each side. *6th row—*Fifteen small Med each side of middle, 3 half Med beyond at each side. *7th row—*One small Med in middle, 19 each side of middle, 1 half Med at each end. *8th row—*Three Ch sts with first 2 and last 2 thds of small Med each side the middle Med, 6 Ch sts with middle 2 thds. Repeat at alternate Med. *9th row—*One large Med below middle small Med, using 6 thds from above and 2 ch thds at each side. Seven such Med at each side, alternating with groups of ch. At each end, 3 Med enclosed with single bar. In the next row of Med (7 around the centre back) one 45-inch thd is mounted on the inner thds before the ch thds are knotted in. and where chains are joined a 45-inch thd is added. Wherever a bar juts out beyond the

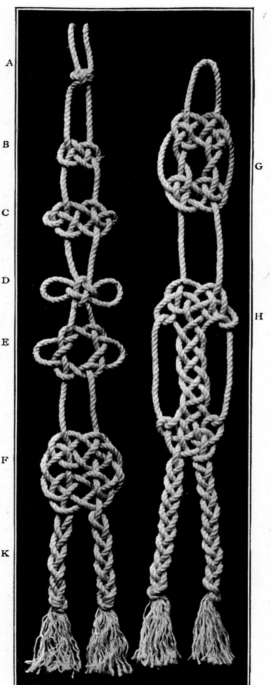

A

B

C

D

E

F

K

G

H

FIG. 31. JAPANESE KNOTS. See page 11

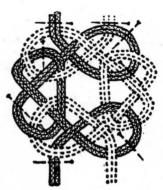

DETAIL OF FIG. 31 F

DETAIL OF FIG. 31 G

DETAIL OF FIG. 31 H

FIG. 30
DETAIL OF
FIG. 31 K

12

work above, a thd has been added (2d mount). Below the Med, pairs of thds are chained 5 times and decreasing to reach the twist border. Outside the first twist, 1½ Ch sts are made, then another twist (see Square for Bedspread, No. 754). Five points at the back have two rows of twist, but as the front is reached the work narrows down and only one twist finishes the edge.

No. 752. Table Scarf.—For this scarf are required 6 balls Macramé cord, No. 12, and ½ yard linen, 48 in. wide. To make the insertion, which is 5 in. wide, cut 32 lengths 3 yds each. Do not double, but tie (temporarily) in groups of 2, 12, 4, 12, 2. Tie about 12 in. from the end. Make 1 Ch st with first and last groups, 1 Fl-st with group of 4 in the middle, 1 Ch st with each pair of these 4 thds, 1 Fl-st with each group of 12, tying with 4 thds over 8. Double Diag Bars to right and left enclose the large Fl-sts. One Ch st with each pair of cords and a Fl-st joins the two ch, which are separated afterward and 1 Ch st is made with each pair. With the 12 thds that fall in the middle, make 5 Fl-sts of 4 thds each. Make 1 Fl-st with the 8 thds in the middle, tying with 2 in each hand. Then 5 Fl-sts below complete the diamond, which is enclosed by Dbl Diag Bars. With the 6 thds that fall at the left, * make 3 Ch sts with the 1st and 2d, with the 6th make 2 binding K close together and pin down, with the 6th as cord make a bar to the left and back to the right *. Repeat from * to *. Repeat the Ch st and binding K again and make a Dbl Diag Bar to the left over the 7th and 8th thds. Make 1 Ch st with the two cords. Repeat this work at the right. In this scarf, 16 scallops make the band 48 in. long. The ends (which should be at least 12 in. long) are joined in a Hor Bar, the cord of which is 27 in. long, and the bar in the middle of the cord. At each side are added 22 thds, 24 in. long, doubled, making 44 ends. These are mounted like Fig. 5. Each pair of thds is employed in 2 Ch sts, 2 pairs are joined with a Coll K, and each pair is knotted with 2 Ch sts below. The thds that fall from the insertion may be disposed of in the same way, or tied in Fl-sts, as these were. After a Hor Bar, entirely across, the thds are grouped in eights and tied in tassels. Three thds, 9 in. long and 1 thd 12 in. long are hung in and the tassel tied with 3 Coll K made with the 12-inch thd, and the tassel cut 4 in. from the last bar. The first end is finished in the same way. For the medallions, which measure 4 in. across, cut six 2-yd lengths, tie a binding K in the middle of one. Pin down the K at the left and make 2 Hor Bars to the right over the cords with the other 5 thds, drawing these thds to the middle. With the left thd that falls make another bar to the right, knotting also with the previous cord. Repeat this with the left hand thd remaining. Unpin the work and pin the K above (so the bars are vertical) and make two bars down at the right to correspond. Make 3 Ch sts with the two upper thds at the left and 2 Ch sts with the next two. Cut four 27-inch thds, tie a K in the middle and pin one down at the end of the outer Ch st, make over the two ends, a Dbl Bar,

using the 6 thds that fall. Add another 27-inch thd and repeat the bars. Let these cords fall, do not K them. Make 3 Ch sts with 2 outer thds, 2 Ch sts with next two. With the 6th as cord make 3 Hor Bars to the left, using the right thd as cord and knotting on the previous cord. Make a binding K of the 3d cord and make 3 bars to the right, 3 Ch sts with 2 outer thds and 2 Ch sts with next two thds. Leave the left side for the present and make the right side to correspond. With the 8 thds that fall within the medallion, make 2 Ch sts with each pair, tie the 4th and 5th thds in a Coll K. With the 4th as cord make a Cordon st with the 3d, 2d, and 1st. Pass the first back under the cord and make a Cordon st, leaving first at the outside of the little circle. Reverse this at the right over the 5th thd. Then with the 4 thds inside the circle make a Cordon st with 2d over 1st, and with 3d over 4th. Tie a Coll K in the centre and make a Cordon st with 1st over 2d and with 4th over 3d. Complete the circular bar by knotting these thds and tie the two cords in a Coll K. Reverse the work

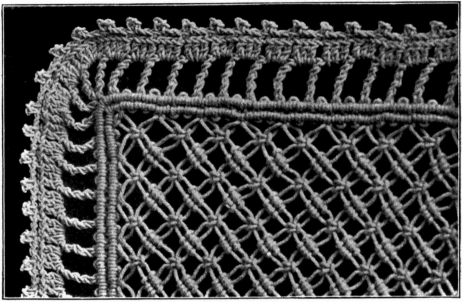

No. 751. SECTION OF PILLOW COVER. See page 11

for the rest of the medallion and fasten underneath.

Figure 41. Fringe. — This fringe (see page 33) is made of the same thd as the gimp, Fig. 40, on page 32. One hank, or two balls, will make a yard. The thds are cut 45 in. and doubled, mounted (1st mount), over a dbl cord the desired length. A Hor Bar follows. Two alternating rows of Fl-st are followed by another bar. Two rows of Fl-st, alternating, follow below the bar. Beneath the first 7 Fl-sts make 6, beneath 6 make 5, beneath 5 make 4, continue until there is but 1 Fl-st. Make these points throughout. With the 8 thds that fall from the point, make 2 Dbl ch of 6 sts. Tie these and make a tassel by looping the remaining thds (see Fig. 42). The other figure of 16 thds is made with—* a Coll K with the 2 middle thds, Diag Bars to right and left, letting the cords hang *. Repeat until there are 6 bars. At the left make chains of 11, 9, 7, and 5 sts with 4 pairs of thds. Reverse at the right. Unite these 16 thds with 2 Fl-sts made with 2 thds in each hand. Below, Dbl Ch each 4 thds 10 or 12 sts and tie of uniform length.

No. 753. Waste Paper Basket. *Materials.*— Seven balls of écru Macramé cord, No. 12; 1½ gross kindergarten beads; 3 dozen ½-inch wood beads; a

13

[84]

No. 752. TABLE SCARF. See page 13

common wire basket and some dark material to cover the wire frame, wine-colored felt or any dark-colored cotton. The frame is covered first, and the Macramé cover made over that. The fringe is made separately, and crocheted around the top to the cover already pinned on the basket. Forty-eight inches in circumference at the top, 30 inches at the bottom, and 12½ inches high are the measurements.

On a dbl cord, pinned around the top, are mounted 30 thds cut 2 yards long and doubled, spaced about 1½ in. apart. These 60 thds are tied in 6 rows of Fl-st, each row an inch below the preceding row. The 7th row is tied 2½ in. below the 6th row. The lower band of work measures 4 in. deep. A Dbl Bar is made around, and after each group of 4 thds joins the bar, 4 thds (cut 1 yd long and doubled) are mounted (2d mount). This requires 60 lengths of 1 yd each. Now there are 180 ends to make 20 figures of 9 thds each. To make the figure: Take 9 thds, * with the 9th as cord make a Diag Bar to the left, knotting on the 8th, 7th, 6th, and 5th. Then with the 1st as cord make a Diag Bar to the right, knotting on the 2d, 3d, 4th, and the cord that comes from the right *. Repeat from * to * twice and thread a bead on the 5th and 6th. Make 20 figures in the 1st row. For the 2d row, take 4 thds at the right of a group above and 5 thds of the next group to the right for each figure. And for the 3d row do the same. A Hor Bar follows and "binding off" (see Fig. 19) finishes the bottom. A fringe of 48 in. for around the top is made as follows: Cut 162 thds 2 yds long, double and mount (2d mount). Make 2 Dbl Ch sts with each group of 4 thds. A Hor Bar follows, then 2 rows of 36 figures. In the 3d row make 3 figures, in the 4th row 2 figures, in the 5th row make 1 figure. Thread a bead on the 5th and 6th thds of each figure throughout. With the 7 thds that fall where the figure is omitted, in the 3d row, thread one of the large wood beads, and these, together with the next groups that fall at either hand are tied in a tassel. The long thds are looped over before it is bound with 5 Coll K. When cut there will be 48 ends 4½ inches long. Make 9 Ch sts with the 2 thds that fall from the point below the last bead, thread another bead and below that one of the large wood beads. Tie the thds in a binding K and cut close to the K. With the outer thread at left and at right make 8 Dbl bh sts over the next 2 thds. There are now remaining 8 thds; with 4 in the middle make a Coll K, with 2 in the middle thread 1 bead, make 6 Ch sts, thread a bead and a large wood bead, tie and cut. The ends that hang are to be turned to the back of the work, sewed securely and cut.

Figure 32. Insertion with Mitred Corner.—Figure 32 is intended for a framelike border or hollow square for Table-cover or Bedspread. In the gray Macramé cord, of which it is made, it measures 4½ in. wide. Thirty thds are cut 42 in. long then doubled and mounted (1st mount). A Hor Bar is made with half the thds, then a thd of the same length is mounted on the bar (2d mount) and the foundation cord is turned at right angle. Draw a right angle on paper, A B C, and another, E D F, 4½ in. from the first, a diag line, B D, and pin this to the cushion, pinning the work to these lines. The pattern that follows is made in this way: *1st row*—* A Coll K with the 4th and 5th thds, 8th and 9th, 12th and 13th, etc. To the left and right of each K is made one Cordon st *. *2d row*—A Coll K with 2d and 3d, 6th and 7th, 10th and 11th, etc., and a Cordon st each way. *3d row* —Like 1st, then Coll K like 2d row and a Hor Bar. At the Diag line, 2 doubled thds are added over the 2 thds at the corner, making a Flat-st with the loops.

In this little border 6 thds are added, making 12 thds for use. Three doubled thds are mounted over the cord, one at the corner and one each side of the next single thd. The diamond pattern follows below the bar. * One Cordon st, with 4th as cord, 3 chain (ch) sts with 5th and 6th, 4 ch sts with 7th and 8th, 3 dbl ch sts with 9th and 10th, and 11th and 12th, and afterward 1 ch st with each pair of these 4. Four ch sts are made with 13th and 14th, 3 ch sts with 15th and 16th, 1 Cordon st, using 17th for cord and 18th for knotting. Tie 19th and 20th in a Coll K. Repeat from *. Going back to the left, make a Diag Bar to the right over the 1st thd, a second bar to the right, using 2 more thds at the right end. Two ch sts with 1st and 2d bar to the right over 3d, taking up 2 more thds to the right.

With the 2 thds that fall make 2 ch sts, bar to the right, using 2 more thds to the right. With left thd as cord make a bar to the right, knotting with 3 thds (the third is the cord from above), * 2 ch sts with 2 thds that fall, 1 Cordon st, using cord from above for knotting. When the next 10 thds are worked in reversed order to this point, tie a Coll K with the 2 cords. Going back to the left, make a Dbl Diag Bar to the right with the first 6 thds, tie a Coll K with 6th and 7th thds. Then fill the half diamond with 7 linen sts. It is enclosed by 2 Diag Bars to the left, and the rest of the band reverses the work of the upper half. Then it is all reversed at the right. A Hor Bar and the upper border pattern repeated below are followed by another Hor Bar. The "binding off" (see Fig. 19) matches as nearly as possible the mount of the upper edge of the insertion. The Diag line may be mounted and pinned down to the line on paper. Two Coll K are made with the 2 thds at the corner, then lay the middle of 2 added thds under these 2 corner thds and make a Dbl Bar, making 3 coils instead of 2. Two Coll K follow. Nine times, this imitation or substitute for the twist is made and supplies ends to complete the design at each side of the corner. Each pair of thds for the diagonal may be cut a little shorter, perhaps two inches shorter for each group of four.

Number 754. Square to Match Insertion, Figure 32.—This piece is 9½ in. square. It is mounted with 4 thds (1st mount) cut 64 in. and doubled, the cord tied in a ring. Cut 8 more thds the same length. Make a surrounding bar, mounting 2 doubled thds at each corner by simply hanging, without the 2d coil. Make another bar and at each corner add a doubled thd. Outside this bar there should be 10 thds on each side.

No. 753. Waste-Paper Basket. See page 13

Tie Coll K with 1st and 2d, with 5th and 6th, and with 9th and 10th, on all four sides. Tie one pair at the corner with Coll K and add thds at the Diag as directed for the insertion. Continue this pattern until it is 4½ small diamonds deep, when a surrounding bar is made and the same pattern follows as described for the insertion. Outside the next bar, the border is only one small diamond deep. The edges are finished with a double bar and the ends are to be buttonholed underside as in the "binding off," Fig. 19. This square is intended for use in a table-cover or bedspread, one in each corner or at intervals to suit one's fancy. But it makes a very pretty centrepiece to leave the ends without binding off and cut evenly for fringe.

Number 755. Hand Bag. *Materials.*—One bunch tinsel cord (36 yards), ½ yard black silk, ½ yard black velvet, 2 yards black velvet ribbon (1 inch wide), 6 ivory rings (No. 16), and buttonhole or purse twist to crochet the rings. The bag measures 9 in. wide and 11 in. deep.

Cut 16 thds, each 2¼ yards long, double and mount 8 of them, pinning down the loop as seen at the top of the bag in the illustration. *1st row*—Four Flat-sts. *2d row*—One Coll K, 3 Flat-sts, 1 Coll K. *3d row*—Four Flat-sts. *4th row*—Four Flat-sts directly beneath those of the 3d row. *5th, 7th, 9th, and 11th rows*—Like 2d row. *6th, 8th, 10th, and 12th rows*—Four Flat-sts. *13th, 15th, and 17th rows*—One Coll K, Dbl Bar, 1 Flat-st, Dbl Bar, 1 Coll K. *14th and 16th rows*—Four Dbl Bars. *18th row*—Four Flat-sts. Make another such piece with the other 8 thds. Tie the fringe, cut 4 in. long and tie a tight knot at the end of each thd. Of the cuttings make 2 tassels for the centre of the bottom of the bag. The draw-strings are of

velvet ribbon run through the beading of 2 Flat-sts, and through the crocheted rings sewed along the middle top of the bag.

Number 756. Hand Bag. *Materials.*—One bunch (36 yards) tinsel cord, ½ yard silk and sateen for lining. The bag measures 8½ in. wide and 11 in. deep.

To make a beading around the top, cut one 48-in. and one 96-in. length. Tie a Coll K with the middle of the longer over the middle of the shorter thd. Pin down the K so that 4 ends fall, the two longer outside the shorter. ✻ About ¾ of an inch below tie a Coll K with the outer thds over the 2d and over the 3d. Pin down these K an inch apart, and bring all 4 thds together in a Flat-st ✻. Repeat from ✻ to ✻ until there are 12 such sections. This is sewed around the top, catching the Coll K only to the silk. The cords for draw-strings are 4-strand sennit (see

C   F

A   B

E   FIG. 32. INSERTION AND MITRED CORNER. See page 14   D

Fig. 24, B). Cut 2 lengths, 4½ yards each, this should make 1½ yards, which will make both strings. For the triangular section across the bottom, cut 4 lengths 36 in., 4 lengths 33 in., 4 of 30 in., 4 of 27 in., 4 of 24 in., 4 of 21 in., and 8 of 18 in. With 2 of the longest cords, tie a Coll K in the middle of both and pin down. Tie (as for the beading) a Coll K ¾ of an inch below and pin knots an inch apart. Before draw-

both triangular sections down with the last K 2 in. apart and pin this last made K half way between to connect both sections. The same work repeated will join the other edges.

One row of Flat-sts all around and a Coll K with each pair of thds completes the piece which is to be sewed to the silk bag. The end of each thread should be tied in a tight knot.

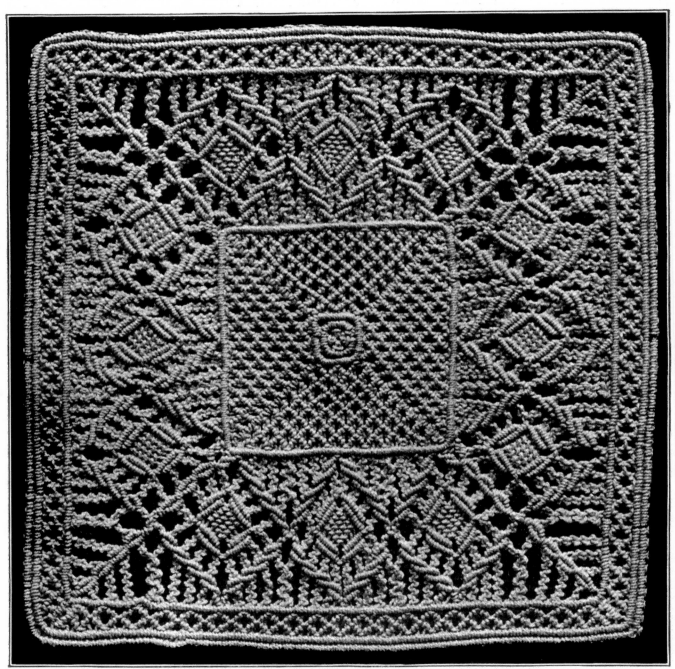

No. 754. SQUARE FOR BEDSPREAD OR CENTREPIECE. See page 15

ing these knots close, insert a thread of the next shorter length, drawing it to the middle. Make a Flat-st with 4 middle thds. Tie at each side, Coll K as before and insert the next shorter length thd, drawn to the middle. Keep on widening in this way until 6 thds have been added at each side and there are 5 Flat-sts between. Make below another row of 6 Flat-sts. Now with the remaining thds make another such section, leaving 4 thds of 18 in. Tie a Coll K with the middle of one over the middle of another. Pin

Number 757. Hand Bag. *Materials.*—Eight dozen yards champagne silk cord, 4 dozen yards brown silk cord, 4 strands (100 each) dark red wood beads, and silk or sateen for lining. The bag measures 8 in. wide and 6½ in. deep.

When thds are cut ready to knot on, the ends may be moistened with library paste, which will prevent untwisting of the thd. A bit of paste on the last ½-inch, with the thd twisted to a point, will make it possible to string the beads. Cut 36 2-yard lengths

17

of champagne cord and 24 2-yard lengths of brown cord. Cut 1 40-inch length of champagne, double it and pin across the cushion for a foundation cord. Knot on (1st mount) 6 thds of champagne, 6 of brown, until there are 5 sections. This makes one side, and to repeat it will make both sides in a flat web, which is to be folded together and joined as directed below. The design is in blocks, alternately with and without beads. Each block requires 12 thds, the first one is beaded. * Thread 3 beads on each of the 2d, 5th, 8th, and 11th thds. Make a Flat-st with 1st and 3d over 2d. Push a bead up close, a Flat-st, a bead, a Flat-st, a bead, and a Flat-st. Repeat this process from * with the 4th, 5th, and 6th thds, with the 7th, 8th, and 9th, and with the 10th, 11th, and 12th thds. The knotted block is made with 12 thds. A Dbl Diag Bar to the left is made, using the 5th thd for cord and afterward the 6th for cord. A Dbl Bar to the right is made with the 8th as cord and afterward the 7th as cord, letting the cords fall. A Flat-st is made with the 8 thds that fall within the bars, 2 thds in each hand tied over with 4 middle thds. Again the cords are taken up (the inner thds first), and Dbl Bars made to the right and left. A Hor Bar is made entirely across the work after each row of blocks. After the last bar is finished, the work may be taken from the cushion and folded together, wrong side out, the cords at each end lapped and overcast firmly for an inch on the wrong side of the work. Then turn right side out, and for the fringe tie 6 thds (3 of the front and 3 of the back) in a binding K.

After the fringe is tied, cut it to a length of 6 in. from the last bar. The straps are 42 in. in length, each one is made as follows: On a cord of 48 in., string 39 beads. Cut a thd 10 yards long, double, and secure the doubled end and cord. If the cord can be stretched it will facilitate the work greatly. The two long ends, wound on a piece of cardboard, will serve as a shuttle, and a very small safety-pin to hold the thread at convenient length, is useful. Make 11 Flat-sts, * a bead, a Flat-st, a bead, a Flat-st, a bead, 12 Flat-sts. Repeat from * until there are 13 groups of beads, then finish with 11 Flat-sts. Sew the straps inside the top of the bag and finish with a lining of brown silk. To stiffen the top with a bit of whalebone is a very good plan.

Number 758. Hand Bag. *Materials.* — One bunch (36 yards) tinsel cord, 1 yard figured ribbon, ¾ yard plain ribbon, 8 ivory rings No. 16 and Pearl cotton No. 5, or silk twist for crocheting the rings. It measures 7½ in. wide and 11½ in. deep.

In this bag, No. 758, a panel of Macramé is mounted over a band of dark silk, the rest of the bag is a figured silk. A band of Macramé is carried across the bottom and the draw-strings are of tinsel cord. For the panel, cut 8 2-yard lengths, mount by pinning 4 loops of the doubled cord, and make for the *1st row*—Two Flat-sts. *2d row*—One Coll K, 1 Flat-st, 1 Coll K. Alternate these two rows for 15 rows. Make a second panel like the first. Pin them down, leaving twice the width of one panel between the two. Cut 16 thds, each ½ yard long. In line with the last row of panel, mount

No. 755. Hand Bag of Black Velvet and Tinsel Cord. See page 16

8 ½-yard lengths. These are mounted as follows: Tie a Coll K at the middle of 2 thds and pin down at 4 points between the two panels. A row of Flat-sts is made across, beginning with the middle of the panel. An alternating row of Flat-sts is made below. Then the second edge of the bag is finished by joining the other two edges of the panels, with a border made of the remaining 8 ½-yard lengths. This is sewed to the silk bag and hard knots tied in the ends of fringe after it is trimmed evenly. Eight ivory rings, No. 16, are crocheted with green Pearl cotton, No. 5, and sewed near the top for the drawstrings. To make the draw-strings, cut 4 3-yard lengths. For one string, double 2 thds and make 4-strand sennit (see Fig. 24, page 9), commencing 4 in. from the end and leaving 4 in. at the last, and these ends will form the tassel. A binding K before and after the braid will keep this from raveling. Make the second cord in the same way. When the drawstrings are in place, through the rings and panel, then the knots may be untied and 8 ends tied together.

Number 763. Tassel. — Cut 4 thds, each 1 yard long. Pin the centres side by side in a vertical position and with the left thd as cord make a Dbl Hor Bar to the right. Now pin the work again so the bar

stands vertically and make a Dbl Diag Bar, using the same cord throughout, turning it at the inside and outside of the ring. Work to the left and right in this way until there are 8 points at the circumference. Let the ends fall together. Tie the 2 middle thds in a Coll K, the middle 4 in a Flat-st, and a Flat-st over 4 thds with 2 at each side. With the 2 outer thds make zigzag st, 8 bars. Buttonhole one of the 4 middle thds over the other 3. Tie and hang in 16 thds 8 in. long (see Fig. 42, page 34). Bind the tassel and cut 3 in.

Number 759. Buttons. —

Number 759, A is made of écru Cordonnet crochet cotton, No. 2, and requires about 8 yards of thread. Cut 18 thds, each 15 in. long, using 6 thds make 3 Hor Bars over 3 thds, bringing the block of bars in the middle of all the thds. Add 3 thds at each side and make a block of 3 bars above and 3 below, and at the left and right of the centre block. These bars should all be at right angle to the centre block. * Make 2 Flat-sts with 4 thds that fall at each corner, then left and right triple Diag Bars, using middle 2 thds for cords. Weave 4 thds that fall from the bars *. Repeat from * to * all around. Then with the 3 thds remaining at the middle of each side, make 2 Flat-sts. Tie a Coll K with the first of these 3 and the thd to the left, also with the 3d of these

No. 756. HAND BAG OF TINSEL CORD AND BROCADE. See page 16

No. 757. Silk Cord Bag. See page 17

and the thd to the right. Below make 3 Ch sts with each pair.

Number 759, B.—This is made of Pearl cotton, No. 5, and dark green glass beads, mounted over green corded silk.

The addition of the beads is the only difference between No. 759, B, and No. 761, A.

Number 761, A (see page 23).—Cut 14 lengths, each 15 in. long, of écru Cordonnet crochet cotton, No. 2. Tie a Coll K with the middle of 1 thd over the rest, separate in 4 groups of 7, with the right thd of each group as cord make a Dbl Diag Bar to the left, and with both cords make 3 Ch sts. With 4 thds that fall from the bar make a Flat-st. With 2 of these thds, at the right, and the ends from Ch st at the right, make a Flat-st. With 2 at the right beyond this, and 2 at the left of the next Flat-st, make a Flat-st, including the single thd, tying over 3 thds.

Number 761, B.—Two thds 12 in. long, 2 of 10 in., and 2 of 8 in. are required. Double the 12-inch thds and pin down the loops side by side, an inch from the loops make a Flat-st. A 10-inch thread, doubled, is pinned a little distance each side of the first loops. In the *2d row* there are 2 Flat-sts. An 8-inch thread, doubled, is pinned at each side and 3 Flat-sts make the *3d row*. Two Flat-sts in the *4th row*, and 1 in the *5th row* completes the net or web that covers the button.

Number 761, C.—Cut 16 thds 15 in. long, double, and mount on a cord 8 or 10 in. long; draw the cord into a ring and tie tightly. Pin the ring on a cushion and separate the thds into groups of 8. * With 4 thds in the middle of the group, make 1 Flat-st, then 3 Diag Bars to the left and right. Repeat from * around. With the 1st and 2d thds, make 2 Ch sts, weave the 3d, 4th, 5th, and 6th, and make 2 Ch sts with each pair. Make 2 Ch sts with the 7th and 8th thds. After finishing the other 3 groups to this point, make a Flat-st with the last 2 thds of one group and the first 2 of the next group to the right.

Number 760. Lamp Shade.

Materials.—Five balls écru Cordonnet crochet cotton, No. 2, 1 small skein old blue Pearl cotton, No. 5.

The shade measures 32 in. in length and 7 in. deep. There are 20 sections of the fringe, for each section cut 10 thds 1½ yards long. Mount with picot heading and Hor Bar. *1st row* —Divide the thds in groups of 4, make a Cordon st with 2d over 1st, then a Dbl Bar to the left, using the 4th thd for cord each time, and a Cordon st with 4th over 3d. A Hor Bar follows and a second bar 1 inch below this, these thds are woven in groups of 6 with the old blue Pearl cotton. Repeat the 1st row and finish with a Dbl Hor Bar. With 20 thds make 1 section of the fringe. Leaving the first 4 thds, with the 12 middle thds make 6 chains — the 1st of 3 Ch sts, the 2d of 2 Ch sts, and the 3d of 1 st; reverse this order for the 4th, 5th, and 6th. Make a Coll K with the 2 middle thds and make Dbl Bars (over 6th and 7th thds) to the left and right. After making 2 Ch sts let the thds fall. Tie the 2 middle thds in a Coll K about ⅛ of an inch from the last bars and make Dbl Bars to the left and right again, making 3 Ch sts with the thds and let them fall. Again make a Coll K, and left and right single bars, then 5 Ch sts and let the thds fall. With the first 4 and the last 4 thds, make a framework of intersecting bars to enclose the point already completed, letting 2 thds fall outside and using the inner thds as the work reaches them. Alternate sections of the fringe are tied with Pearl cotton, to make a tassel. The weaving or darning of the inch-deep band near the top is done with the same color, in groups of 6 thds. The remaining thds are knotted at intervals. The Macramé work is mounted over China silk.

Figure 33. Fringe.

—Macramé cord (the size of Cordonnet crochet cotton, No. 2) was used in this model. Thirty-six thds, doubled (72 ends), are required to make one point. It is mounted with Venetian picot.

Cut 2 thds 1 yard long, 2 thds 1 yard and 6 in. Increase the length of each pair by 6 in. until the length of 2 yards and 12 in. is reached. Cut 4 thds of that length, then decrease 6 in. for each succeeding pair, until the length of 1 yard is reached, cut 4 altogether of 1 yard and increase as before. *1st row*—Diagonal bar to the right with 6 thds. *2d row*—Horizontal Bar, followed by 3 bh sts with the 3d over 1st and 2d,

No. 758. Silk Bag with Tinsel Cord. See page 18

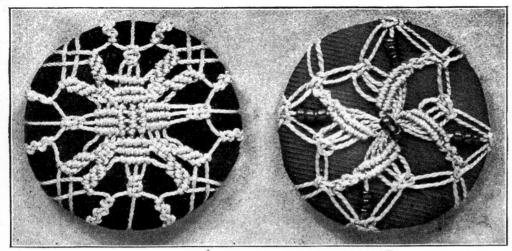

A

A   B
No. 759. MACRAMÉ COVERED BUTTONS.   See page 19

and 6th over 4th and 5th. *3d row*—Three bh sts made with 5th over 3d and 4th thds, and with 8th over 6th and 7th. *4th row*—Horizontal Bar followed by Dbl Diag Bars to the right with groups of 6 thds. *5th and 6th rows*—Like 2d and 3d. * Diagonal triple bars to the right with 1st group of 6 thds, the same to the left, and tie the two middle thds in a Coll K *. Repeat from * to * the whole length. With 5th, 6th, 7th, and 8th thds of each group of 12, make a shell of 6 Flat-sts (see Fig. 22, A, page 9). When 6 shells are finished, make below: 5 pairs of triple bars and 5 shells, 4 pairs of triple bars and 4 shells, 3 pairs of triple bars and 3 shells, 2 pairs of triple bars and 2 shells, 1 pair of triple bars and 1 shell.

Number 762. Bag. —This bag is 8 in. wide and 10½ in. deep. Fringe, 3½ in. Draw-strings, 1 yard each.

Materials. — Eighty yds tinsel cord and ½ yd green silk for lin-ing. Cut 8 lengths of 2 yds and 12 in., 4 lengths of 2 yds and 10 in., 4 of 2 yds and 8 in., 4 of 2 yds and 4 in., 4 of 2 yds, 4 of 1 yd and 32 in., and 4 of 1 yd and 29 in. For draw - strings cut 4 lengths of 3 yds.

The bag should be worked on a round, firm cushion, as it is made in one piece. The threads are mounted by pinning down the loops (as seen in illustration). The longest threads are mounted on the two sides of the cushion, which are to be used for front and back centre of the bag, the lengths grading toward the edge.

1st row—Sixteen Flat-sts. *2d row*—Sixteen Flat-sts, alternating with those above. *3d row*—Like 1st row. *4th row*—Four bh sts with each pair of thds. *5th row*—Sixteen Flat-sts. *6th and 7th rows*—Alter-nating Flat-st. *8th row*—Four medallions (med) in centre of front and back. These med are made of 5 med knots (see Fig. 34), and Flat-st to complete the row. *9th, 10th, and 11th rows*—Sixteen Flat-sts. *12th row*—Two med below 2 middle med above, and Flat-st to complete the row. *13th, 14th, and 15th rows*—

No. 760. LAMP SHADE. See page 21

22
[93]

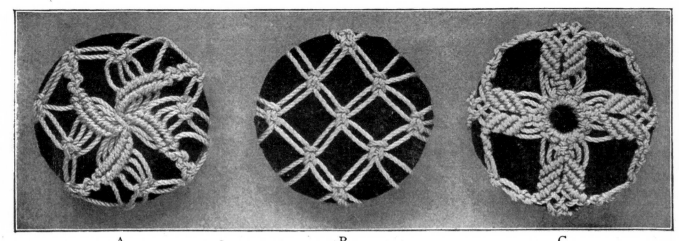

A   B   C

No. 761. MACRAMÉ COVERED BUTTONS. See page 20.

Flat-st. *16th row*—Seven Flat-sts at each side of the bag. *17th row*—Six Flat-sts. *18th row*—Five Flat-sts.

Fringe.—Both sides knotted together in two rows single thds cut 3½ in. and finished by a hard knot.

Draw-strings.— Four-strand sennit (see Fig. 24, page 9).

Number 764. Centrepiece or Cushion Cover.—This piece is 15 in. square, not including the fringe, and is made of seine twine. It is commenced at the centre, and threads are added almost constantly to keep the corners filled. Cut 18 threads (thds) 3 yds long; place two of them together and tie a knot (k) at the middle. These are the 4 cords that start from the centre. To each of these, 4 thds are added, each 3 yds long. Draw a thd (to the middle) under the cord, make 1 Cordon st over the cord. Add 3 more thds in the same way, and repeat this with all four cords. Make a second bar close to the first, using the first cord as last knotting thread. There are now 8 thds at each side, beside a cord at each corner. Cut a 10-inch thd, double, pin down the loop at one corner, make a bar all around the work, using every thd and making the corners as nearly square as possible. With a crochet-hook draw the ends of this cord through the loop and sew down neatly at the back of the work.

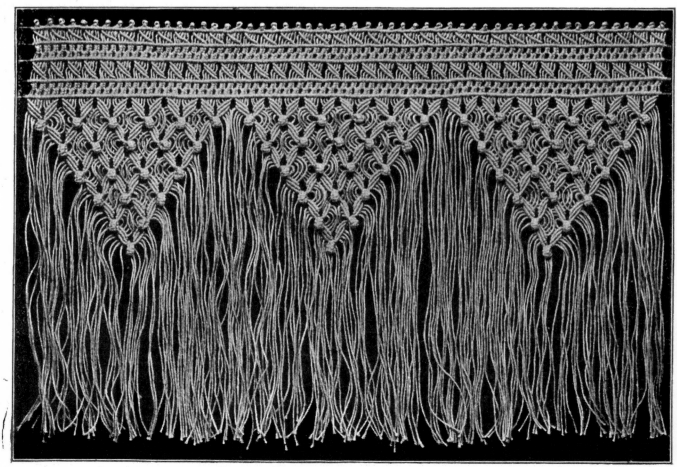

FIG. 33. VANDYKE FRINGE. See page 21

No. 762. POMPADOUR OF TINSEL CORD. See page 22

4 in the middle. Around the square, now make another bar, adding at each corner 6 thds, doubled, and mounted in second mount. Outside the bar, midway of each side, is one Flat-st, after which the thds divide and each pair makes 4 Ch sts. The 4 thds on each corner make 2 Ch of 3 sts each and go on toward the corner in a network of Ch that to describe would only be confusing. Where one chain branches, the extra thds are added by knotting them on each thd of the chain. The large square at the corner has 8 Flat-sts on each side, requiring 16 thds at each side; as but 6 thds are furnished by the 3 Ch, the others must be added on the first cord, 5 thds doubled will make the number. The design between these squares is clearly shown. Two bars are made before the border. On these bars are added 8 thds (16 ends) at each corner. For the border, the thds are divided in groups of 4, two groups making one figure. When making the last Dbl Bar, 4 thds (8 ends) are added near each corner, at both sides of the corner figure. Each tassel is made of 8 thds, the two outer thds making 2 Flat-sts over the others, after which they are tied together at the back and sewed down.

No. 763. TASSEL
See page 19

Number 765. Basket.—This basket is 8½ in. in diameter, 25½ in. around, and about 4 in. high. The material is Macramé cotton No. 20. The work is started at one side, and a band of work (like an insertion) made long enough to reach around the basket and joined at the side by sewing. Cut 26 thds, each 6 yds long, double and mount (2d mount. *1st row*— Letting the first 4 thds hang, * make 4 Diag Bars to the right with 8th, 7th, 6th, and 5th as cords and 9th, 10th, 11th, and 12th as knotting thds. Make 4 Diag

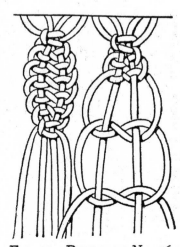

FIG. 34. DETAIL OF No. 762

Make another bar in the same way, adding a single thd (one end only) at each corner. Then make right and left Dbl Bars with the 8 thds at each side, the middle 2 thds tied in a Coll K, and left and right Dbl Bars bring that figure to the third bar. On each of the two cords at the corners, mount 3 doubled thds (second mount), with ends toward the corner, and make a second bar close to the mount. With 8 thds in the corner make a Flat-st, 2 thds in each hand over

Bars to the left with 17th, 18th, 19th, and 20th as cords, and 16th, 15th, 14th, and 13th as knotting thds, letting ends and cords fall *. Repeat from * to * twice more, or 3 times in all. *2d row*—With 1st 8 make 1 Flat-st, 2 thds in each hand over 4. With 9th to 16th, make 4 Hor Bars with 9th as cord, back and forth; with 17th to 24th a Flat-st; with 25th to 32d, 4 Hor Bars with 25th as cord; with 33d to 40th, Flat-st; with 41st to 48th, 4 Hor Bars with 41st as cord; with 49th to 52d, 2 Hor Bars to the right, using left thd each time as cord. With the same 4 thds, make 2 Hor Bars to the left, using the right thd each time as cord. This completes the little point at the top of the basket (the top is at the right hand). In working the 3d row, the Diag Bars are to the left and then to the right. And in the 4th row, the first thread at the left is the cord for the Hor Bar. The handle is covered with bh st.

Number 766. Card Case.—This measures, when closed, 3¼ x 4⅜ in. It is made of crochet cotton No. 5. Cut 68 thds 1 yd and 6 in. long. Do not double, but mount within an inch of the middle on a Hor Bar, one Cordon st with each thd. Make 1 row of Flat-st and another Hor Bar. Leaving 1st and last 4 thds, make 6 figures of 10 thds each. * Tie a Coll K with the 5th and 6th thds, using these as cords for Diag Bars to the left and right. Tie a Coll K with 2 middle thds and make bars as before, letting the cords hang. * Continue this until but 2 thds are left. Make 5 more such figures, interlocking the outer cords of each figure with the next. With 4 thds at each edge, make Fig. 26, E, page 10. Interlock the bh thd with the cord of the figure next it. Repeat until there are 7 rows of figures, and make the other half of the case in the same way. Close with crocheted button and loop of Ch st.

No. 764. Centrepiece or Pillow Cover. See page 23

25

[96]

Number 768. Bag.—This bag measures 7 in. wide and 11 in. deep, including handle and fringe. The thd is a twine of about the size of Cordonnet crochet cotton, No. 2, and requires 3 balls. Cut 46 thds 3 yds long, and place side by side for making the handle. These will be called padding (pad) threads. Cut 2 thds 5 yds long and place with the others, having the middle at the middle of the bunch. From this point work Flat-st with the 2 long thds, over the bunch. Work each way until the handle is 7½ in. long. Divide each end into two even parts, taking from the pad thds for knotting thds and allowing the first knotting thds to fall with the bunch. Work Flat-st over each part for 2½ in., making the purl edge come at right angles to that on the first, or top, part of the handle. With 4 pad thds form a shell where the threads divide to become points for the top of the bag. Divide the thds again, when there should be 12 thds in each group. Add 4 new thds (8 ends) by looping them over a thd at the back of the work and allow 4 ends to go with each group. * Take 2 thds from a group for knotting and make 3 Flat-sts over the others. Let fall a pad thd from each side *. Repeat from * to * until only 4 thds remain. Work the other points down in the same way. Join the points by tying 2 knotting thds (one from each point) in a Coll K. These points are filled in with Flat-st, 1st row with 1, then 2, then 3, etc., until all the thds have been used. Below the points make 8 more rows

No. 766. Card Case. See page 25

of Flat-st, followed by bars of 7 Spiral sts. Then there are 4 rows of Flat-sts, followed by another row of Spiral Bars. Three rows of Flat-sts, then narrow the work by omitting 1 st at each side of the bag, for 6 rows. Using 2 thds from each edge of the bag as cords, make a Hor Bar to the middle of the bag. Taking the 2 that are now at the edge of the bag, for cords, make another Hor Bar. Sew these cords at the back of the work and cut.

The remaining thds are knotted in Dbl Ch st an inch or more, after which each group of 4 Ch is drawn together with 2 Flat-sts, forming a tassel. The bag is lined with satin.

Number 767. Card Case.—This measures, when closed, 4⅝ in. by 3⅜ in. It requires 1 ball of écru Cordonnet crochet cotton, No. 2. Eighteen thds, each 1 yd long, are doubled and mounted with Ch p, around a ring ¾ of an inch in diameter. Outside the Dbl Bar, 2 Ch sts are made with each pair. Eighteen thds, each 34 in. long are mounted (with Ch p), 1 after each Ch. The Dbl Bar measures 1½ in. outside. Ten thds at each end and 26 thds at each side make the figures shown in the illustration. At the surrounding bar, 9 thds (18 ends) are added at each corner and 2 thds (4 ends) added between the figures at the sides.

Number 769. Collar.—Use linen Macramé cord, No. 6, 3 balls. Cut 80 thds, each 2 yds long. Mount with single thd picot on Hor Bar, or rather a circular bar. Collecting knot with 4th thd

No. 765. Macramé-Covered Basket. See page 24

No. 767. CARD CASE. See page 26

illustration, much of it is Ch st. One thd 1½ yds long is to be added for the first bar, or added at the lower point of the square. This makes the right grouping below; 20,—22,—20, thds for the tassels. It measures 15 inches long.

Number 772. Fringe.—This fringe is 7 in. long and 13 in. deep, and requires 42 thds doubled (84 ends). Cut 6 thds 1½ yds long, 12 thds 1 yd and 12 in, 12 thds 1 yd and 6 in, 12 thds 1 yd long. Mount 6 of the shortest thds first, 6 of the next, etc. They are mounted with Ch P followed by a Dbl Bar. Twenty-one groups of 4 thds form triple bars to the right, etc. Two balls will make this section.

Number 773. Belt. *Materials.*—One ball gray Pearl cotton, No. 3; 1 string wood beads. Cut 16 thds 6 yds long, doubled, making 32 ends. For the bh loop, find centre of 4 thds and make 8 Flat-sts. Make two more such loops, leaving 4 thds simply doubled. Fold one loop and pin on the cushion, with left thd for cord, make

over 1st, 2d, and 3d, followed by a bar. Divide thds in groups of 8 (see detail, Fig. 36, page 29). In making the 3d bar, 10 thds, doubled (20 ends) should be added. At the 4th bar are added 10 thds, 18 in. long, doubled, making 20 ends. For the jabot cut 10 thds 2 yds long (see detail, Fig. 35, page 28).

Number 770. Hat Ornament. *Materials.*—One ball gray Macramé cord, or Pearl cotton, No. 5; 44 dark blue beads and 44 ochre beads. Cut 12 thds 1 yd long and pin down in the middle all together. Make a circular bar, adding 12 thds that are cut 20 in. and doubled, mounting one after every pair of thds. One Cordon st with each pair of thds all around, 1st over 2d as cord. A circular bar, adding 12 thds, ½ yd long, doubled, mounting one after every 4 thds. On each 6th thd string a blue bead, make a Coll K with 2d, 3d, and 4th of the 5 thds of a group. Repeat around. Make a circular bar, then with each group of 6 thds make a Diag Bar to the right, another to the left, meeting in the centre. String an ochre bead on the 1st thd, a blue bead on the 3d, and an ochre bead on the 6th. Make Dbl Bars right to centre and left to centre. Of the 3 thds that fall at the side of the last bars, make a square block of 3 bars, with these and the next 3 thds. String an ochre bead on centre thd at left, a blue bead at right, tie underneath and fasten by sewing down.

Number 771. Medallion.—This Medallion, No. 771, and Fringe, No. 772, on page 30, and Circular Medallion, No. 775, on page 31, have much in common, and are used for trimming evening wraps, etc. The material is écru Cordonnet crochet cotton, No. 2, 1 ball is required. Cut 30 thds 1½ yds long, double, and mount in 15 groups of 2 each on two sides of a 2½-inch square.

A P K and 2 Flat-sts are made in the middle of each group, these pinned down and mounted on a Dbl Bar. The work can be followed from the

No. 768. BAG WITH POINTED TOP. See page 26

a Hor Bar of the remaining 7 thds. Add 2 more doubled thds to continue the bar. Add another bh-loop and continue the bar with these 8 thds. Add the 2 remaining thds on the bar and finally add the last loop, carrying the bar to the end. With the same cord make the bar to the left and the work is ready for the design. * With 1st 4 thds make Dbl Diag Bars to the right, and with the next 4 thds make Dbl Diag Bars to the left. String 1 bead on 4th and 5th thds, make Dbl Bars to the left and to the right *. Make from * to * three times more.

A Dbl Hor Bar over 1st thd follows. Make triple Diag Bars to the right with 1st 8 thds, the same to the left with next 8 thds, joining 8th and 9th with a Coll K. Repeat with last 16 thds. String 1 bead on the 16th and 17th thds. Reverse the Diag Bars and string 1 bead on the 8th and 9th, and 1 on the 24th and 25th thds. Finish last section with beads to correspond with first, make 8 lines of 8 Flat-sts and finish the under-lapping end with a Dbl Bar and binding off (see Fig. 19, page 7). Crochet 3 buttons to fasten with the loops.

Number 774. Hair Band.—This measures 26 in. in length and 1½ in. wide, and requires 21 yds of tinsel cord. Cut 2 lengths 5 yds each and 2 lengths 5½ yds each. Double and pin down in loops as for Bag No. 763, page 24, placing the 2 shorter thds at each edge and the 2 longer thds between. Chain stitch, Flat-st, and medallions are employed, which are all shown at No. 762, page 24, and Fig. 37, detail of No. 774, on page 31.

Number 775. Medallion.—This medallion, for trim-

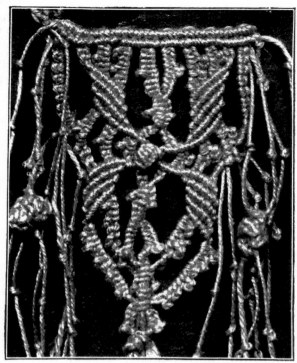

FIG. 35. DETAIL OF No. 769

No. 769. COLLAR AND JABOTS. See Figs. 35, 36, and page 26

FIG. 36. DETAIL OF COLLAR, NO. 769
page 28

ming an evening wrap, is made of écru Cordonnet crochet cotton, No. 2, 1 ball.

Cut 5 thds, each 30 in. long, pin down together in the centre, spreading the ends out evenly. Cut 1 thd 2 yds long for knotting thd. Knot around the centre twice, making 1 Cordon st over each radius, or spoke. Add 10 thds, 30 inch, doubled; 1 pinned down with small P between 2 spokes. This gives 30 thds for cords. Knot around twice more. Add 15 thds, 30 inch, doubled; 1 pinned down with P within each pair of spokes. Two rows of Flat-st all around, 2 rows of Flat-st, dividing the st of previous row. Add 18 thds (18 inch and doubled) at the circular bar, in 3 spaces mount 2 thds instead of 1. Add 60 thds, 15 in. long and doubled, at the outer Dbl Bar. Fifty-four pairs of thds around the top are knotted with Ch st,

NO. 770. HAT ORNAMENT. See page 27

NO. 771. MEDALLION TASSEL. See page 27

29

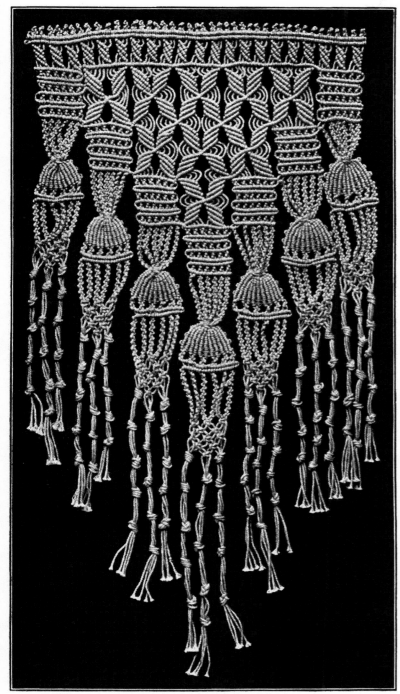

No. 772. FRINGE. See page 27

folded and sewed. The others are chain stitch, varying from 6 to 36, and finished with a large bead.

Number 776. Hat Trimming. — Two balls of medium size (No. 9), Macramé cord are required. For the band, cut 32 thds, each 3 yds long. Do not double, but knot them, temporarily, at the middle in groups of 6,—10,—10,—6. The working detail, Fig. 39, beginning in the middle, is very clear, and to be repeated to the end of the thds. Then turn and work the other half to correspond. This will make about 24 in. For the ornament, Fig. 38, cut 18 thds, each 2 yds long, using 9 doubled thds for each "crown." Beginning at the right of the right crown,—over 1 doubled thd, make a Dbl Hor Bar with 4 doubled thds (2d mount). Make 4 more Dbl Bars, spreading as they appear in the cut, and turning the work each time. With the last cord make a Dbl Bar with the 9 cords that fall. In making this bar, make 3 coils for each thd. With the remaining 9 thds make a crown that is reversed. At this point

No. 773. BELT. See page 27

30

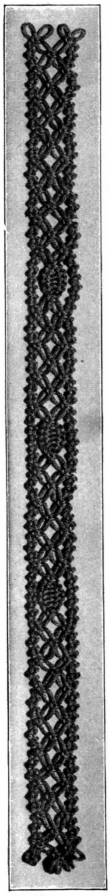

No. 774
HAIR BAND
See page 28

the crowns are to be pinned in the position at Fig. 38, and the work is easily followed from there.

Number 777. Bag.—Two balls of écru Cordonnet crochet cotton, No. 2, are required. Cut 41 thds 1¼ yds long, double and mount (1st mount) and make a Hor Bar. This measures 5½ in. Make a Coll K with the 6th and 7th thds, also with the following pairs,—16th and 17th,—26th and 27th,—36th and 37th,—46th and 47th,—56th and 57th,—66th and 67th,—76th and 77th. Make a Flat-st with the 2d, 3d, 4th, and 5th, 2 Flat-sts between knots and 1 Flat-st with last 4 thds. Letting the 1st thd fall, make a Ch st with 2d and 3d, 1 Flat-st below each 2 Flat-sts above, and Ch st with last 2 thds. Make a bar to the left, using 6th for cord, and a Coll K with cord and 1st thd, a bar to the right with 7th as cord. Repeat this the entire length, knotting the last cord with the last thd that falls. Tie Coll K as before with the cords. In each diamond of this row, 1 Flat-st of 8 thds is made. In the next row there are 4 Flat-sts of 4 thds each. Tie the tassels with 3 thds in each hand, looping the remaining thd to have 18 thds in each tassel. If necessary, thds can be added before the tassel is tied with Coll

No. 775. MEDALLION WITH BEADS. See page 28

FIG. 37. DETAIL OF HAIR BAND. See No. 774

No. 776. HAT TRIMMING. See Figs. 38, 39, and page 30

FIG. 39. DETAIL OF BAND NO. 776

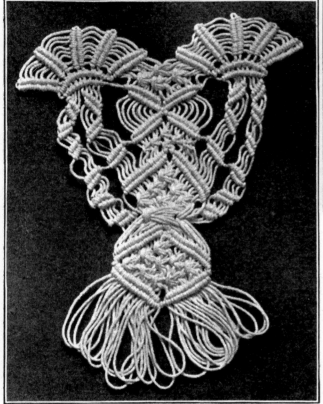

FIG. 38. DETAIL OF No. 776

K (see Fig. 42, page 34). Make two such pieces and sew to a black velvet bag.

Number 778. Dress Garniture.—Use Cordonnet crochet cotton, No. 3. A sleeve trimming 14 in. long accompanies this garniture. No illustration of it is given, it being a straight band with the same design

as the yoke. The following directions are given for the straight band: Cut 12 thds, four 4-yd lengths, four 3½-yd lengths, and four 3-yd lengths. Knot in the following order, with Dbl Bar on a short thd doubled—2 of the longest, 2 of the next length, and the 4 shortest thds in the middle, then 2 longer and 2 longest, giving 24 working thds. With the first 4 thds at the left, make 6 Flat-sts, and the same with the last 4 thds. With the 9th and 10th (held together) as cord, make a Diag Bar to the left, using the first 8 as knotting thds. With the 11th and 12th (held together) as cord, make a second bar to the left with the same knotting thds. With the 4 cords, make 3 Flat-sts. Make the right half to correspond and tie a large Flat-st, 4 thds in each hand over 8 thds in the centre. With the 4 thds at the left, as cords, make Diag Bars to the right, using 8 knotting thds that fall from the centre Flat-st, and with the first 4 of these make 7½ Flat-sts. Then with the 4 thds at the right, as cords, make a Dbl Diag Bar entirely across the work, always remembering to take the cords double. After 7½ Flat-sts are made with 4 thds at the right, a Dbl Diag Bar to the right is made with the 15th and 16th, and the

FIG. 40. INSERTION OR APPLIQUE. See page 35

32

[103]

13th and 14th as cords. This length of thd makes a band 14 in. long, 13 diamonds altogether.

To make the yoke and jabot, the thds may be cut ¼ longer, or thds may be tied at the back, and after the work is finished, pick out the knot and sew the ends down neatly. The work of the yoke is like the straight band for the sleeves, except that the inner edge has but 6 Flat-sts and the outer edge has 9 Flat-sts. If any change is made in the length of this yoke it must still have an uneven number of diamonds, on account of the jabot. It is added after the yoke is made, and requires 48 thds, which, when doubled and mounted, give 96 ends. For each side cut 12 lengths 40 in., and for the middle cut 24 lengths 50 in. Mount these as follows: With a crochet-hook, draw one end of a thd up through the outer edge of a Flat-st and down at the next Flat-st. Draw the next thd up in the same place, the last one passed down. The manner of working is the same as for the yoke and sleeves, except that where the cords meet they are tied in a Flat-st, using 8 thds. The bottom of this is finished with tassels, as shown in the

No. 777. Velvet Bag with Fall of Macrame. See page 31

Fig. 41. Fringe. See page 13

33

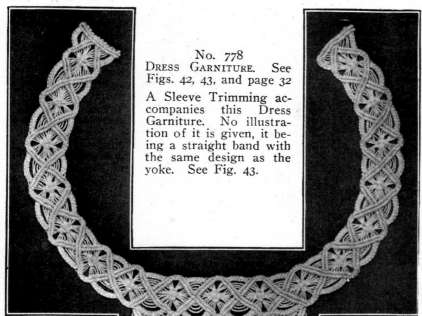

No. 778
DRESS GARNITURE. See Figs. 42, 43, and page 32

A Sleeve Trimming accompanies this Dress Garniture. No illustration of it is given, it being a straight band with the same design as the yoke. See Fig. 43.

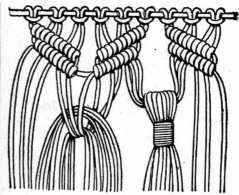

FIG. 42. DETAIL OF TASSEL, NO. 778

illustration (see also Fig. 42). Extra thds are added to each tassel to cover the knot and to make them heavier. The winding of each tassel is done with a thd used in a darning-needle, so it can be passed down through the tassel to fasten it. The yoke measures 18 in. and the tassel a little over 4 in.

Number 779. Handkerchief Bag. — This bag measures 6 x 6½ in., and requires 2 balls gray Macramé cord (No. 6) and 4 dozen Ivory rings, No. 12. The thds are cut long enough to make both sides, the piece folded at the bottom, and while finishing the second side, the two are joined by Coll K at each edge. Cut 20 thds, 3 yds long, double and mount (2d mount), in 4 groups of 5. After each group slip a ring on the cord. Make a second bar. Then follow left and right Diag Bars, while with 2 Coll K the rings are attached. To make the chains: With 2 thds 4 yds long, 12 or 14 in. of single ch, in the middle of the thds. Run this ch through the 8 rings at the top of the bag. With 4 thds coming out at one edge of the bag, make Dbl Ch 5 in. * Slip a ring on the left thds and tie 3 Ch sts, pass the right thds down through the ring and tie 4 Ch sts *. Repeat until 5 rings are used. Separate the thds and make single Ch with each pair 5 times and tie the ends in a tassel. Make another Ch and bring the ends out at the other edge of the bag. Instead of adding rings work through those on the first Ch and finish with a tassel as before.

Number 780. Hand Bag. — Any hand-bag can be covered with a net of Macramé, as No. 780, page 35, by having a pattern of one side and half each end of the bag. Mount (1st mount) rather openly on a doubled cord, more than twice the length all around the top, measured with the mouth of the bag open. Alternating rows of 2 Flatsts make the net. When the pattern for one side is covered, repeat and join the last edge with the work pinned on the bag. A Hor Bar all around and the thds tied inside will finish the bottom. Two balls of écru Cordonnet crochet cotton, No. 2 covered this bag, which measured 7 in. wide.

Number 781. Fan Bag. — This Bag measures 3 x 8 in., and requires 1 ball écru Cordonnet crochet cotton, No. 2, and 3 dozen ivory rings, No. 8. To make the bag, cut 16 thds each 3½ yds long. Make 6 Ch sts with the middle of each pair for the Ch P mount. When the Dbl Bar is finished with 16 ends, make 4 Ch sts with the two cords before mounting the other section. Make right and left Dbl Bars, Coll K where bars come to a centre, and 2 Coll K to attach the rings. The first lozenge, or diamond, is filled with "quadrilled threads" (simple weaving with double threads), in the others a Coll K unites the 8th and 9th thds. At the bottom make a Dbl Bar across both sections, between sections make 3 Ch sts. Fold the work, and in making the second side of the bag join both at the edges with Coll K. When the top is reached, make

FIG. 43. DETAIL OF NO. 778

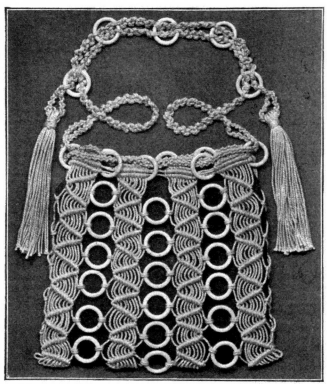

No. 779. HANDKERCHIEF BAG WITH IVORY RINGS.
See page 34

ends down inside the bar. For the handle or strap: Cut 2 thds 3¼ yds, fold and mount in one ring at the edge, then make 18 Flat-sts, * join in a ring, 6 Flat-sts, *. Repeat from * to * until 8 rings are used, then finish with 18 Flat-sts and join to the ring at the other edge.

Number 782. Bag.—This beautiful bag, No. 782, is unique in several respects. It is made of blue Pearl cotton, No. 3, and the piece of work is made twice the depth of the bag and folded at the bottom, the sides being closed by sewing. The work-

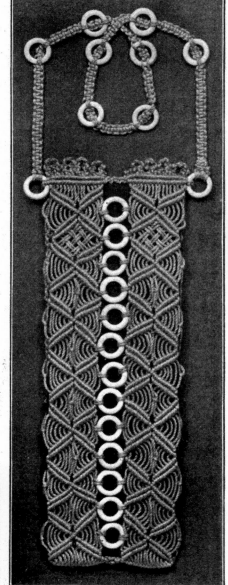

No. 781. FAN BAG WITH IVORY RINGS.
See page 34

a Dbl Bar over the original foundation cords, slipping a ring over the Ch sts at each edge. Chain, (5 times) the alternate pairs of thds and sew P and thd

No. 780. HAND BAG WITH ALL-OVER NET OF MACRAMÉ. See page 34

ing model, Fig. 45, shows the mounting about half down one side. The side requires 54 thds, doubled (108 ends). The work is given so clearly that it need not be described in detail. It begins with from 5 to 8 alternating rows of Flat-sts. While the exact length of the thds cannot be given, it would be well to cut 12 or more thds 2½ yds long. After knotting these the necessary length can be ascertained. The fringe is made separately (Fig. 44), and two rows sewed to the fold. The ends are knotted together.

Figure 40. Insertion or Appliqué.—This is made of

Pearl cotton, No. 3, the color is called "gray wood" or "gris-bois." It is 1¾ in. wide, and 1 hank will make 4½ yds, or 1 ball will make half as much. Cut 8 lengths of 6 yds, double and mount on a short cord. Make a Hor Bar across over the 1st thd. Down the centre make 2 Ch sts with 7th and 8th also with 9th and 10th, a Dbl Diag Bar to the left with these 4, and 2 Ch sts afterward with each pair. At the left make * 3 Ch with 1st and 2d, 2 Ch with 3d and 4th, 1 Ch with 5th and 6th, Dbl Diag Bar to the left and to the right with these 6, 6 Ch with 1st and 2d, 4 Ch with 3d and 4th, 2 Ch with 5th and 6th. From * reverse the work at the right. Make a Dbl Diag Bar to the left with the first 6 over the 7th and 8th thds. Reverse at the right. Then follows a block of 9 Flat-sts, enclosed by Dbl Bars. In alternate blocks there is a Flat-st made with 12 thds, 2 at each side tying over 8. Repeat as from the first with this exception, a l w a y s (after the starting) the Ch sts are 6, 4, and 2.

Figure 46. Insertion with Mitred Corner.— One ball of Pearl cotton, No. 3, will make a half yard of this insertion, Fig. 46, 4½ in. wide. Cut 16 thds 42 in. long, double, making 32 ends, and mount (1st mount). When making the bar add 2 doubled thds (2d mount) at the corner. Draw two right angles, A B C and E D F, 4½ in. between, and at B draw a Diag to D. Begin at A, when B

No. 782. HAND-BAG OF BLUE PEARL COTTON.   See page 35

is reached the additional thds may be pinned down to the line B D. A piece of blotting-paper, so marked, and pinned to the cushion will keep the work square. *1st row*—Flat-sts of 4 thds. Mount an additional thd at each side after each Flat-st in the diagonal. Each pair of thds in the mitred corner is graded. Cut 8 thds 40 in., 8 thds 38 in., and each group of eight 2 in. shorter than the preceding group. *2d row*—Flat-sts alternating with 1st row. *3d row*—Like 2d. *4th row*—Like 2d. *5th row*—Like 1st. *6th row*—Horizontal Bar. The thds for mounting and bars should be long enough to allow for the whole length desired, whether two sides and one corner, or four sides and four corners. *7th row*—Flat-stitches with 5th, 6th, 7th, and 8th, with 17th, 18th, 19th, and 20th, etc. *8th row*—Flat-stitches with 3d, 4th, 5th, 6th, and with 7th, 8th, 9th, 10th, etc. *9th, 10th, 11th, and 12th rows*—Flat-stitch throughout. Below the 12th row the work divides in groups of 6 thds. * Flat-stitch with 3d, 4th, 5th, 6th, then with 1st, 2d, 3d, 4th *. Repeat from * to * 5 times, then take the second group of 6 thds and make Flat-st * with 1st, 2d, 3d, 4th, then

FIG. 44. DETAIL OF FRINGE, NO. 782

FIG. 45. DETAIL OF HAND-BAG, NO. 782. See page 36

with 3d, 4th, 5th, 6th, *. Repeat from * to * 4 times and 1 Flat-st with 1st, 2d, 3d, 4th. Then reverse the work from the 12th row back to the 1st row, and bind off at the outer edge.

Number 783. Square.—This square measures 8 in., and requires 1 ball of Pearl cotton, No. 3. Cut 16 thds of each of the following measures: 45 in., 42, 40, 36, 32, 28, 24, 20, 18, using them in that order. Mount 8 thds (1st mount), doubled, in a ring, add 2 at each corner on the bar (2d mount). Make 8 Flat-sts, and at each corner mount a doubled thd on each outer thd that falls from the Flat-st. Continue diagonals until 5 have been added. Along each of the four sides of the square make the border of Fig. 46, page 38. From this point on directions for one side only are given. Outside the bar follow pattern of Fig. 46 for 6 rows. *7th row*—Two Flat-sts below each 3. *8th row*—One Flat-st below each 2, and 1 Coll K of 8 thds between. *9th row*—Two Flat-sts below 1. *10th row*—Eight Flat-sts. *11th row*—Seven Flat-sts. *12th row*—One Flat-st with first 4 also with last 4, and 2 Flat-sts with middle thds. *13th row*—Collecting knot with 8 thds, Flat-st, Coll K with 8. *14th row*—Two Flat-sts in the middle. *15th row*—Three Flat-sts. *16th row*—Two Flat-sts. *17th row*—One Flat-st. After the three other sides are finished to this point a bar is made all around and the diagonal line starts from the point of each side. From this bar the border of Fig. 46 is made, and another bar. Each group of 4 is tied in a Coll K. At the corners thds are mounted to fill out the square. A Dbl Bar follows all around and it is bound off (see No. 754, page 17.)

Number 784. Hand Bag.—This

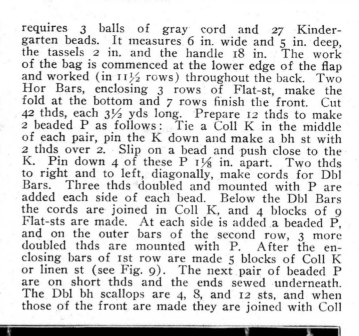

requires 3 balls of gray cord and 27 Kindergarten beads. It measures 6 in. wide and 5 in. deep, the tassels 2 in. and the handle 18 in. The work of the bag is commenced at the lower edge of the flap and worked (in 11½ rows) throughout the back. Two Hor Bars, enclosing 3 rows of Flat-st, make the fold at the bottom and 7 rows finish the front. Cut 42 thds, each 3½ yds long. Prepare 12 thds to make 2 beaded P as follows: Tie a Coll K in the middle of each pair, pin the K down and make a bh st with 2 thds over 2. Slip on a bead and push close to the K. Pin down 4 of these P 1⅛ in. apart. Two thds to right and to left, diagonally, make cords for Dbl Bars. Three thds doubled and mounted with P are added each side of each bead. Below the Dbl Bars the cords are joined in Coll K, and 4 blocks of 9 Flat-sts are made. At each side is added a beaded P, and on the outer bars of the second row, 3 more doubled thds are mounted with P. After the enclosing bars of 1st row are made 5 blocks of Coll K or linen st (see Fig. 9). The next pair of beaded P are on short thds and the ends sewed underneath. The Dbl bh scallops are 4, 8, and 12 sts, and when those of the front are made they are joined with Coll

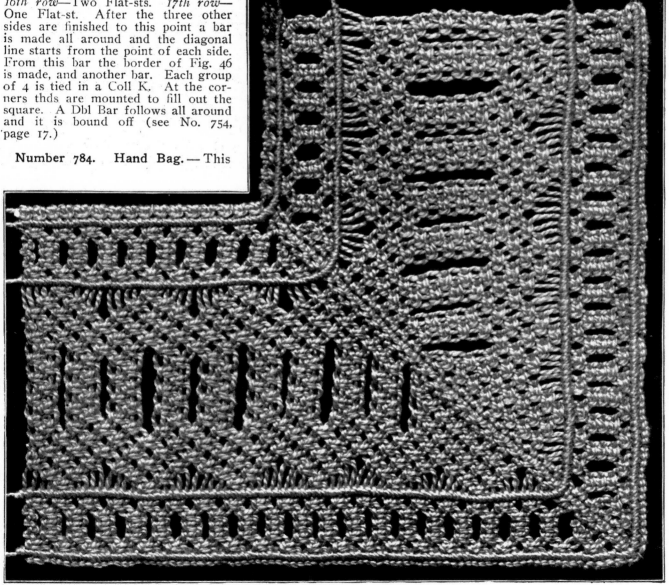

FIG. 46. INSERTION AND MITRED CORNER. See page 36

38

K to those of the back. Six thds 25 in. long make one tassel. Tie a binding K at the middle of 6 thds, a Flat-st of 3 thds at each side over 6, pass the 12 ends through a bead. Below the bead, cast aside the two outer thds and make Flat-st of 8 thds. Cast aside 2 as before and make Flat-st of 4 thds. Double bh the remaining thds in 5,—8, and 10 s.s. Draw these ends through the work at the fold and fasten

Macramé is adapted to so many purposes, made in such a variety of materials, and made in so many different grades of work, that its use should be widespread. The difficulty of the work varies, from that a child will pick up eagerly and accomplish to that possible only to the skilled, experienced worker.

The waste-paper basket, on page 15, and table-scarf, on page 14, represent the coarsest grade of material

No. 783. Square to Match Insertion, Fig. 46. See page 38

inside. This is easier accomplished before finishing the front of the bag. This bag furnishes a good example of Linen-stitch or Collecting Knot, in the diamond filled with that stitch. A more compact or durable piece of work can scarcely be imagined. Used in a mass, to cover a considerable space, this stitch forms a firm, thick fabric not often found in the realm of needlework. The strap of the bag is made of two double chains. The cords are cut 1½ yards long. At intervals of about 1½ inches a bead is slipped over all 8 threads.

shown in this book, No. 12 Macramé cord; while the fan bag, on page 35, and velvet bag with fall of Macramé, on page 33, employ the finest thread in the book, that is No. 2 Cordonnet crochet cotton. Portières are sometimes made of heavier cords of seine twine, some beautiful examples being found in the work of the Germans and French. Combinations of Macramé stitches and fringe with drawn-work and Hardanger designs on heavy linen canvas, are made by English workers, and some very elaborate and beautiful results are obtained by these combinations.

39

No. 784. MACRAMÉ HAND-BAG WITH BEADS. See page 38

40

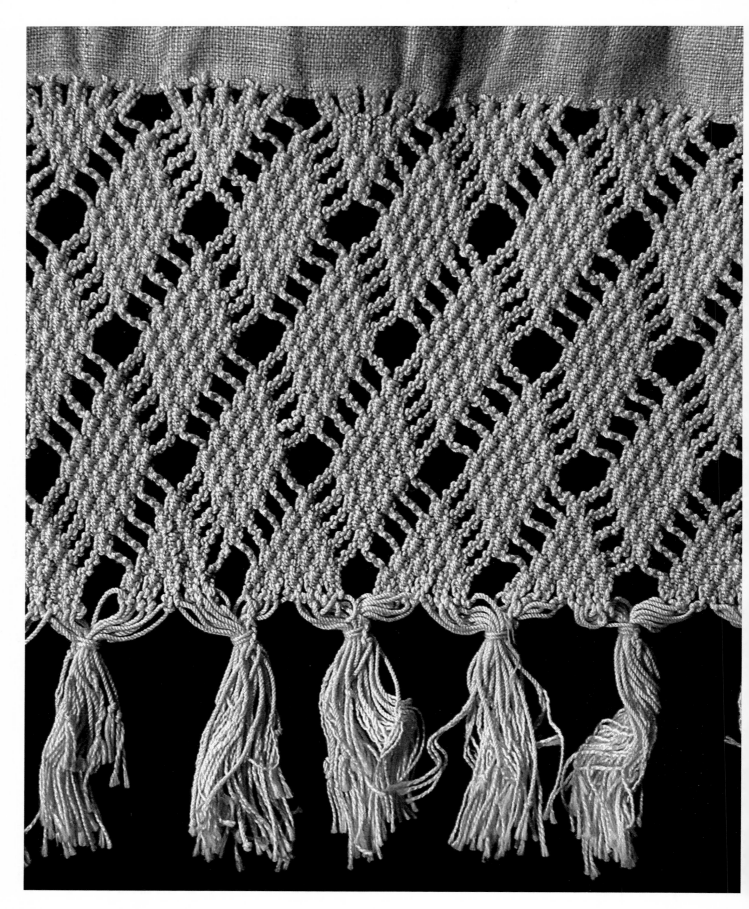

MACRAME TOWEL FRINGE, 19TH C.
from collection of LACIS MUSEUM OF LACE AND TEXTILES [JGG.14745]